MESMERISM
AND THE END OF THE ENLIGHTENMENT IN FRANCE

See p. 5 for description of title page illustration.

MESMERISM

and the End of the Enlightenment in France

ROBERT DARNTON

SCHOCKEN BOOKS · NEW YORK

TO THE MEMORY OF MY PARENTS
AND TO JOHN

PREFACE

This little book has a large purpose: it attempts to examine the mentality of literate Frenchmen on the eve of the Revolution, to see the world as they saw it, before the Revolution threw it out of focus. So presumptuous an undertaking must fail, for who can hope to peer into the minds of men who have been dead for almost two centuries? But it is worth attempting and may attain some degree of accuracy through the use of neglected clues to that mentality, which have been left scattered in the scientific periodicals and pamphlets of the time, in scraps of popular songs and cartoons that were hawked in the streets, in the letters-to-the-editor and paid announcements of publications that one might have found lying about eighteenth-century drawing rooms and cafés, and finally in private letters, diaries, police reports, and records of club meetings that have survived in various manuscript collections. Such material leaves a strong impression of at least the interests of the reading public in the 1780's, and these interests provide some surprising information about the character of radicalism at that time. They show how radical ideas filtered down from treatises like Rousseau's *Social Contract* and circulated at the lowest level of literacy.

Faced with the impossibility of knowing all the topics of interest, even among the elite who left accounts of them, I have limited this study to what seems to have been the hottest topic—science in general, mesmerism in particular. If the reader recoils with a feeling that this may be indeed too surprising, too quackish a subject for his attention, then he may appreciate the chasm of time that separates him from the Frenchmen of the 1780's. These Frenchmen found that mesmerism offered a serious explanation of Nature, of her wonderful, invisible forces, and even, in some cases, of the forces governing society and politics. They absorbed mesmerism so thoroughly that they made it a principal article in the legacy of attitudes that they left for their sons and grandsons to fashion into what is now called romanticism. It is not surprising that mesmerism's place in this legacy has never been recognized, for later generations, more squeamish perhaps about the impure, pseudoscientific sources of their own views of the world, have managed to forget Mesmer's commanding position during the last years of the Ancien Régime. This study would restore him to his rightful place, somewhere near Turgot, Franklin, and Cagliostro in the pantheon of that age's most-talked-about men. In so doing it may help to show how the principles of the Enlightenment were recast as revolutionary propaganda and later transformed into elements of nineteenth-century creeds. It thus may help one to understand how the Enlightenment ended—not absolutely (for some still take seriously the Declaration of Independence and the Declaration of the Rights of Man and Citizen)—but historically, as a movement characterizing eighteenth-century France. It may merely help the reader to taste the flavor of the distant past. But if it achieves this last, more limited objective, it will have been worthy perhaps of his attention; for such tastes provide the pleasure in the study of history.

Much of the pleasure that I have derived from my own studies I owe to Harry Pitt and Robert Shackleton of Oxford University. I would also like to record my gratitude to those who supported me during the preparation of this book—the Rhodes Trustees, the Warden and Fellows of Nuffield College, Oxford, and the Society of Fellows of Harvard University—and to those who read it at various stages of its evolution—Richard Cobb, John Plamenatz, Philip Williams, Crane Brinton, Jonathan Beecher, and John Hodge. With a hospitality that would have delighted their ancestor, the original Gallo-American, the Bergasse du Petit-Thouars family made available to me not only their papers but also the château containing them.

In order to avoid cluttering the page with footnotes, references have been grouped into long notes, in which citations are listed according to the order of the quotations' appearance in the text. Impossibly long eighteenth-century titles have been abbreviated with ellipsis dots. The places and dates of publication of works are cited as they appear on title pages, even in the case of such obvious fictions as "Philadelphia" or "The Moon"; and where the names of authors and the places and dates of publication are not given, they are lacking in the original works. Spelling and punctuation have been modernized, except in citations of titles. I have done the translating and have preferred to render "magnétisme animal" (often shortened to "magnétisme" in the eighteenth century) as "mesmerism," despite the claim of a modern expert, who believes that "mesmérisme" was first used in the early nineteenth century.[1] Actually, the French of the 1780's used it and "magnétisme animal" as synonyms.

Cambridge, Massachusetts   Robert Darnton
April 1968

1. H. S. Klickstein, review of Bernhard Milt, *Franz Anton Mesmer und seine Beziehungen zur Schweiz,* in *Bulletin of the History of Medicine,* XXIX (1955), 187.

CONTENTS

ILLUSTRATIONS

All of the illustrations except the last are from the collections of the Bibliothèque Nationale, Paris, and are reproduced with the library's kind permission. The last illustration is from Louis Bergasse, *Un défenseur des principes traditionnels sous la Révolution, Nicolas Bergasse* (Paris, 1910).

The original French for passages translated in the text may be found in Appendix 7.

MESMERISM
AND THE END OF THE ENLIGHTENMENT IN FRANCE

1. MESMERISM AND POPULAR SCIENCE

The crashing failure of the *Social Contract*, Rousseau's least popular book before the Revolution,[1] raises a problem for scholars searching for the radical spirit in the 1780's: if the greatest political treatise of the age failed to interest many literate Frenchmen, what form of radical ideas *did* suit their tastes? One such form appeared in the unlikely guise of animal magnetism or mesmerism. Mesmerism aroused enormous interest during the prerevolutionary decade; and although it originally had no relevance whatsoever to politics, it became, in the hands of radical mesmerists like Nicolas Bergasse and Jacques-Pierre Brissot, a camouflaged political theory very much like Rousseau's. The mesmerist movement therefore serves as an example of the way in which, on a vulgar level, politics became enmeshed with fads, providing radical writers with a cause that would hold their readers' attention without awakening that of the censors. To explain the radical strain in mesmerism, it is necessary to examine Mesmer's theory in relation to the other interests of the time, to trace the course of the mesmerist movement, and to consider the character of the mesmerist societies. It should then be possible to enjoy an unexpected view of the prerevolutionary radical mentality, a view freed from the overgrowth of quack pamphlets, memoirs, and extinct scientific treatises that have kept it hidden.

In February 1778, Franz Anton Mesmer arrived in Paris and proclaimed his discovery of a superfine fluid that penetrated and surrounded all bodies. Mesmer had not actually seen his fluid; he concluded that it must exist as the medium of gravity, since planets could not attract one another in a vacuum. While bathing the entire universe in this primeval "agent of nature," Mesmer

1. Daniel Mornet, "L'Influence de J.-J. Rousseau au XVIIIe siècle," *Annales de la Société Jean-Jacques Rousseau,* 1912, pp. 44–45; Robert Derathé, "Les réfutations du *Contrat Social* au XVIIIe siècle," *ibid.,* 1950–1952, pp. 7–12.

brought it down to earth in order to supply Parisians with heat, light, electricity, and magnetism; and he especially extolled its application to medicine. Sickness, he maintained, resulted from an "obstacle" to the flow of the fluid through the body, which was analogous to a magnet. Individuals could control and reinforce the fluid's action by "mesmerizing" or massaging the body's "poles" and thereby overcoming the obstacle, inducing a "crisis," often in the form of convulsions, and restoring health or the "harmony" of man with nature.

What lent strength to this appeal to the eighteenth-century cult of nature was Mesmer's ability to put his fluid to work, throwing his patients into epileptic-like fits or somnambulist trances and curing them of diseases ranging from blindness to ennui produced by overactive spleen. Mesmer and his followers put on fascinating performances: they sat with the patient's knees enclosed between their own and ran their fingers all over the patient's body, seeking the poles of the small magnets that composed the great magnet of the body as a whole. Mesmerizing required skill, for the small magnets kept shifting their positions. The best method of establishing "rapport" with a patient was to rely on stable magnets, such as those of the fingers and the nose (Mesmer forbade taking snuff because of the danger of upsetting the nose's magnetic balance), and to avoid areas like the north pole at the top of the head, which usually received mesmeric fluid from the stars, and the south pole in the feet, which were natural receptors of terrestrial magnetism. Most mesmerists concentrated on the body's equator at the hypochondria, on the sides of the upper abdomen, where Mesmer located the common sensorium. This practice stimulated gossip about sexual magnetism but not about hypochondriacs, whose unbalanced humors elicited sympathy, not the scorn reserved for *malades imaginaires*. (The *Dictionnaire de l'Académie Françoise* for 1778 explained that the person who suffered from the "vice des

This contemporary cartoon satirizing a mesmerist session shows the "tub" dispensing fluid through its movable iron rods and ropes. The ladies in the center are forming a "chain" or mesmeric circuit, and those at the sides have passed out from overdoses of fluid. Other patients grapple for the "poles" of surrounding bodies, while the mesmerist, depicted by the traditional ass's head of the charlatan, stirs up the séance by fluid emanating from his own supercharged body, and astrological beams communicate influences from outer space.

hypocondres" tended to be "bizarre et extravagant" and upset when left by himself: "Les hypocondriaques sont mélancoliques et visionnaires.") Gossips also found inspiration in Mesmer's apparatus, especially his mattress-lined "crisis room," designed for violent convulsives, and his famous tubs. These were usually filled with iron filings and mesmerized water contained in bottles ar-

A favorable view of a mesmerist session, emphasizing its general atmosphere of "harmony," the physical and moral accord of man and the laws of nature. Mesmerists identified harmony with health and so used music in the treatment of illness. Health, in the broadest sense of the word, was their supreme value. Therefore the children in the center are being educated, not treated for disease: thanks to their early exposure to the "agent of nature," they may grow up to be natural men. Note the "tub for the poor" in the back room.

M. Mesmer, doctor of medicine of the faculty of Vienna in Austria, is the sole inventor of animal magnetism. That method of curing a multitude of ills (among others, dropsy, paralysis, gout, scurvy, blindness, accidental deafness) consists in the application of a fluid or agent that M. Mesmer directs, at times with one of his fingers, at times with an iron rod that another applies at will, on those who have recourse to him. He also uses a tub, to which are attached ropes that the sick tie around themselves, and iron rods, which they place near the pit of the stomach, the liver, or the spleen, and in general near the part of their bodies that is diseased. The sick, especially women, experience convulsions or crises that bring about their cure. The mesmerizers (they are those to whom Mesmer has revealed his secret, and they number more than one hundred, including some of the foremost nobles of the court) apply their hands to the sick part and rub it for a while. That operation hastens the effect of the ropes and the rods. There is a tub for the poor every other day. In the ante-chamber, musicians play tunes likely to make the sick cheerful. Arriving at the home of this famous doctor, one sees a crowd of men and women of every age and state, the cordon bleu, the artisan, the doctor, the surgeon. It is a spectacle worthy of sensitive souls to see men distinguished by their birth and their position in society mesmerize with gentle solicitude children, old people, and especially the indigent.

LE BACQUET DE Mr MESMER,
ou Représentation fidelle des Opérations du Magnétisme Animal.

ranged like the spokes of a wheel. They stored the fluid and transmitted it through movable iron rods, which the patients applied to their sick areas. Sitting around the tubs in circles, the patients communicated the fluid to one another by means of a rope looped about them all and by linking thumbs and index fingers in order to form a mesmeric "chain," something like an electric circuit. Mesmer provided portable tubs for patients who wanted to take mesmeric "baths" in the privacy of their homes, but he generally recommended communal treatments, where each individual reinforced the fluid and sent it coursing with extraordinary power through entire clinics. In his outdoor treatments, Mesmer usually mesmerized trees and then attached groups of patients to them by ropes in daisy-chain fashion, always avoiding knots, which created obstacles to the fluid's harmony. Everything in Mesmer's indoor clinic was designed to produce a crisis in the patient. Heavy carpets, weird, astrological wall-decorations, and drawn curtains shut him off from the outside world and muffled the occasional words, screams, and bursts of hysterical laughter that broke the habitual heavy silence. Shafts of fluid struck him constantly in the sombre light reflected by strategically placed mirrors. Soft music, played on wind instruments, a pianoforte, or the glass "harmonica" that Mesmer helped to introduce in France, sent reinforced waves of fluid deep into his soul. Every so often fellow patients collapsed, writhing on the floor, and were carried by Antoine, the mesmerist-valet, into the crisis room; and if his spine still failed to tingle, his hands to tremble, his hypochondria to quiver, Mesmer himself would approach, dressed in a lilac taffeta robe, and drill fluid into the patient from his hands, his imperial eye, and his mesmerized wand. Not all crises took violent form. Some developed into deep sleeps, and some sleeps provided communication with dead or distant spirits, who sent messages by way of the fluid directly to the somnambulist's internal sixth sense, which was extra-

Another view of a mesmerist séance, which communicates something of mesmerism's stylish, overheated *sensiblerie*. The lady on the right is being overcome with a "crisis." The lady in the background has been seized with convulsions and is being carried into the mattress-lined "crisis room."

ordinarily receptive to what would now be called extra-sensory perceptions. Many hundreds of Frenchmen experienced such marvels, but few if any fully understood them, for Mesmer always kept his greatest doctrinal secrets to himself.[2]

Extravagant as it seems today, mesmerism has not warranted the neglect of historians, for it corresponded perfectly to the interests of literate Frenchmen in the 1780's. Science had captivated Mesmer's contemporaries by revealing to them that they were surrounded by wonderful, invisible forces: Newton's gravity, made intelligible by Voltaire; Franklin's electricity, popularized by a fad for lightning rods and by demonstrations in the fashionable lyceums and museums of Paris; and the miraculous gases of the Charlières and Montgolfières that astonished Europe by lifting man into the air for the first time in 1783. Mesmer's invisible fluid seemed no more miraculous, and who could say that it was less real than the phlogiston that Lavoisier was attempting to banish from the universe, or the caloric he was apparently substituting for it, or the ether, the "animal heat," the "inner mold," the "organic molecules," the fire soul, and the other fictitious powers that one meets like ghosts

2. Some of Mesmer's 27 basic propositions of animal magnetism are reproduced in Appendix 1. The best of the numerous contemporary pamphlets explaining the theory and practice of mesmerism are: F. A. Mesmer, *Mémoire sur la découverte du magnétisme animal* (Geneva, 1779); *Aphorismes de M. Mesmer, dictés à l'assemblée de ses élèves ...* (published by Caullet de Veaumorel, Paris, 1785); the series of letters by Galart de Montjoie, a student of Mesmer's first important disciple, Charles Deslon, in the *Journal de Paris*, February and March 1784 (esp. issue of Feb. 16, pp. 209–216). For examples of the occult tendencies of mesmerism, see A. M. J. de Chastenet, Marquis de Puységur, *Mémoires pour servir à l'histoire et à l'établissement du magnétisme animal* (1784); Tardy de Montravel, *Essai sur la théorie du somnambulisme magnétique* (London, 1785), which supplied the basis of the somnambulist visions Tardy recounted in hundreds of pages of later pamphlets; J.-H.-D. Petetin, *Mémoire sur la découverte des phénomènes que présentent la catalépsie et le somnambulisme ...* (1787), and *Extrait des registres de la Société de l'Harmonie de France du 4 janvier 1787.*

inhabiting the dead treatises of such respectable eighteenth-century scientists as Bailly, Buffon, Euler, La Place, and Macquer. Frenchmen could read descriptions of fluids very like Mesmer's under the articles "fire" and "electricity" in the *Encyclopédie*. If they desired inspiration from a still greater authority, they could read Newton's description of the "most subtle spirit which pervades and lies hid in all gross bodies" in the fantastic last paragraph of his *Principia* (1713 edition) or in the later queries of his *Opticks*.[3]

Not only did the century's greatest scientist speculate extravagantly about mystical Powers and Virtues that his readers might associate later with mesmeric fluid, but he showed great interest in an occult doctor called Bory ("I think he usually goes clothed in green"[4]), who might have been an early incarnation of Mesmer. Berkeley, one of Newton's first opponents, had his own concept of a vitalistic fluid, which, when distilled by evergreen trees, produced a tar water that would cure all diseases. In fact, there were enough fluids, sponsored by enough philosophers, to make any eighteenth-century reader's head swim. It was a century of "systems" as well as one of empiricism and experimentation. "Scientists," often clergymen, pursued "science," often known simply as philosophy, up the Great Chain of Being until it took

3. A letter from A.-J.-M. Servan, undated and unaddressed, in the Bibliothèque municipale, Grenoble, ms N 1761, illustrates how the speculations in Newton's *Opticks*, which were restrained in comparison with those in his correspondence with Robert Boyle, took hold of the mesmerists: "Pourquoi ne pas revenir tout de suite à la belle conjecture que Newton a développée dans l'un de ses ouvrages? Il avoue l'existence d'un milieu beaucoup plus subtil que l'air et qui pénètre les corps les plus denses, milieu qui, par le ressort de toutes ses parties et les vibrations qui en résultent, est l'instrument des phénomènes les plus singuliers de la nature, du feu, de l'électricité, de nos sensations même etc." For the works on eighteenth-century science to which this account is indebted, see the bibliographical note.

4. Newton to Francis Aston, May 18, 1669, quoted in L. T. More, *Isaac Newton: A Biography* (New York, 1934), p. 51.

them beyond physics to meta-physics and the Supreme Being. The Abbé Pluche, one of the most famous of science's pious primitives, did not have to understand the law of gravity to explain the tides: he went straight to the teleological cause—God's desire to help ships in and out of harbors. Newton's own scientific labors included the study of alchemy, the Book of Revelation, and the works of Jacob Boehme. His readers rarely had so firm a grip on what would now be considered scientific method that they could cut the mysticism out of his theories of light and gravity. They often regarded gravity as an occult power, perhaps a relative of the universe's electric soul or of the vitalistic fire that burned in the heart, according to Harvey and Descartes, and that was produced by the friction of blood against arteries, according to more modern theorists. Until Lavoisier laid the foundations of modern chemistry, scientists usually expected to explain all life processes by a few principles; and once they believed they had found the key to the code of nature, they often lapsed lyrically into fiction. Buffon's style has not killed his reputation as a scientist, but Bernardin de Saint-Pierre (who explained that nature divided melons into sections so that they could be eaten *en famille*) now lives only as a figure in the history of literature, although he was also a scientist to eighteenth-century Frenchmen. They read facts where their descendants read fiction.

The progressive divorce of science from theology in the eighteenth century did not free science from fiction, because scientists had to call upon the imagination to make sense of, and often to *see*, the data revealed by their microscopes, telescopes, Leyden jars, fossil hunts, and dissections. That the eye alone could not decode nature seemed clear from scientific observations of mermaids and little men talking in rocks; and that machines need not improve perception followed from reports of fully developed donkeys seen through microscopes in donkey semen. François de Plantade's famous drawing of a little man whom he claimed to have seen in human sperm under a microscope was debated seriously in the first half of the century. Although it was a hoax, it seemed reasonable in terms of preformation theory and no more ridiculous than Charles Bonnet's concept of the encasement (emboîtement) of all individuals in the primeval parent. Epigenesis was not proven until 1828, and until then a veil of fanciful theory hid the reproductive processes of mammals from the scientists' strained sight.

By the end of the century, a legal dictionary permitted itself some doubts about the bastardy case in which a woman claimed to have conceived a child by her husband, whom she had not seen for four years, during a dream. "It is supposed that the night of the lady of Aiguemerre's dream was a summer night, that her window was open, her bed exposed to the West, her blanket disarranged, and that the southwest wind, duly impregnated with organic molecules of human fetuses, of floating embryos, fertilized her."[5] But not everyone dared deny the power of the maternal imagination: what produced the child with the beef-kidney head, if not the images in its mother's mind during the cravings of pregnancy? Linnaeus even illustrated an ejaculation of semen from a pollen grain that he had observed with a microscope, and he went on to explain plant life by reference to a subtle, magnetized fluid and human physiology. Yet he had only seen plants sleep. Erasmus Darwin detected them breathing, moving their muscles voluntarily, and experiencing mother love. Meanwhile, other scientists were watching rocks grow, clams sprout, and the earth secrete many hybrid forms of life. They saw a different world from the one we see today, and they made it out as best they could with the collection of animistic, vitalistic, and mechanistic theories that they

5. Prost de Royer, Dictionnaire de jurisprudence et des arrêts, 7 vols. (Lyons, 1781–1788), II, 74. The Dictionnaire enthusiastically endorsed mesmerism (V, 226–227).

had inherited from their predecessors. As Buffon recommended, they saw with "l'oeil de l'esprit," but it was "l'esprit de système."

Of the many systems for bringing the world into focus, mesmerism had most in common with the vitalistic theories that had multiplied since the time of Paracelsus. Indeed, Mesmer's opponents spotted his scientific ancestry almost immediately. They showed that, far from revealing any new discoveries or ideas, his system descended directly from those of Paracelsus, J. B. van Helmont, Robert Fludd, and William Maxwell, who presented health as a state of harmony between the individual microcosm and the celestial macrocosm, involving fluids, human magnets, and occult influences of all sorts. Mesmer's theory, however, also seemed related to the cosmologies of respectable writers who sponsored a variety of fluids, which they sent swirling through the universe under familiar names like gravity, light, fire, and electricity. Von Humboldt thought the moon might exert a magnetic force, and Galvani was experimenting with "animal electricity" in Italy at the same time that Mesmer used animal magnetism to cure hundreds of persons in France. Meanwhile, the Abbé Nollet and Bertholon and others had discovered miraculous powers in the universal electric fluid. Some scientists reported that electric charges made plants grow faster and that electric eels cured gout. (After being thrown daily into a tub of water containing a large electric eel, a boy recovered from an irregularity in the use of his limbs. The experimenters did not record whatever shocks his psyche received.) Mesmer's own cures, published with elaborate testimonials, spoke more eloquently for his system than his brief and cryptic publications. He was not, after all, a man of theory (his French disciples took care of the system-building), but an explorer who had embarked on uncharted seas of fluid and returned with the elixir of life. Some detected a note of charlatanism in

Mesmer's treatments, but his apparatus resembled the all-popular Leyden jar and the machines illustrated in standard works on electricity, like Nollet's *L'Art des expériences ou avis aux amateurs de la physique* (1770). These amateurs often sent electrical charges through "chains" of persons like Mesmer's and often regarded electricity as a magic potion that would conquer disease and even (as among the clientele of Dr. James Graham's fertility bed in London) help to create life. Moreover, the alliance between charlatanism and conventional medicine had been exposed so often on the French stage that any admirer of Molière might consider Mesmer's techniques less lethal than those of orthodox doctors and barber-surgeons, secure in their faith in the four humors and the animal spirits, and formidable in their arsenal of remedies: purgatives, cauteries, resolutives, evacuants, humectants, vesicatories, and derivative, revulsive, and spoliative bleeding.[6]

To argue that mesmerism did not seem absurd in the context of eighteenth-century science is not to claim that scientific thought from Newton to Lavoisier was a collection of fictions. At the popular level, however, it entangled the ordinary reader in a jungle of exotic *systèmes du monde*. How was he to separate fiction from truth, especially among the monisms that made up the biological sciences? The heirs of the seventeenth-century mathematical and mechanical philosophers failed to give successful explanations of processes like respiration and reproduction, and the forebears of nineteenth-century romantics, al-

6. For contemporary views of the eighteenth century's semimedieval medicine men—who still dealt in "butter of arsenic," had generally fought against the recent practice of inoculation, and swore by bleeding as a preparative measure for childbirth—see J. F. Fournel, *Remontrances des malades aux médecins de la faculté de Paris* (Amsterdam, 1785), and *Observations très-importantes sur les effets du magnétisme animal par M. de Bourzeis . . .* (Paris, 1783). For a thorough, contemporary analysis of the sources of mesmerism, see M.-A. Thouret, *Recherches et doutes sur le magnétisme animal* (Paris, 1784).

though they speculated stirringly about incalculable inner life-forces, failed also. Mechanists and vitalists commonly disguised their failures in fantastic fluids, but as these were invisible, they could be tailored to fit any system, and some penetrating observers felt distressed at the spectacle of general nudity. Joseph Priestley, the greatest defender of invisible, fluid phlogiston, remarked about the general fascination with electricity, "Here the imagination may have full play, in conceiving of the manner in which an invisible agent produces an almost infinite variety of visible effects. As the agent is invisible, every philosopher is at liberty to make it whatever he pleases." Lavoisier noted the same trend among chemists: "It is with things that one can neither see nor feel that it is important to guard against flights of imagination."[7] No such scruples restrained the ardor of amateur scientists and others seeking the newest frontier of Enlightenment. They had been living comfortably with electricity, magnetism, and gravity for generations, but the invisible gases of chemistry had begun to enter their universe only with the great discoveries of the second half of the century. Joseph Black reported finding "fixed air" (carbon dioxide) in 1755; and during the next thirty years, other scientists, notably Henry Cavendish and Joseph Priestley, dizzied their contemporaries by discovering "inflammable" or "phlogisticated" air (hydrogen), "vital" or "dephlogisticated" air (oxygen), and many other wonders that had been floating about in the common air for centuries, unknown to Aristotle and all his successors. The man-in-the-salon's difficulty in assimilating these gases into his view of the world can be judged by an article in the *Journal de Paris* of April 30, 1784, reporting one of the Lavoisier experiments now known to have given the death-blow to the four-element theory. Since the beginning

7. Joseph Priestley, *The History and Present State of Electricity with Original Experiments* (London, 1775), II, 16; A. L. Lavoisier, *Traité élémentaire de chimie, présenté dans un ordre nouveau, et d'après les découvertes modernes,* 3 ed. (Paris, 1801; 1 ed., 1789), I, 7.

of philosophy, men had agreed that water was one of the four basic elements, the journal remarked, but Lavoisier and Meusnier had just shown the Academy of Sciences that it was a compound of inflammable and dephlogisticated air. "It must have cost dearly to accept that water was not water but actually air," it said, and concluded, "We have one less element."

The discovery of these gases cost the journal's readers dearly because it meant the abandonment of a venerable and reasonable way of looking at the world. Their confusion grew as scientists not only seemed to subtract from the Aristotelian elements but also added elements of their own—the vital and dephlogisticated airs as well as the salt, sulphur, mercury, and other "principles" that had accumulated since the time of Paracelsus. The scientists themselves shared in this confusion and called for a "new Paracelsus" to create a "transcendant," "general, philosophical chemistry," but they left the laymen only more bewildered by rushing in with cosmologies to fill the vacuums that their discoveries had created. To increase the confusion, the invisible forces clashing in the void produced repercussions among the reputations that collided in salons and academies; and the attempt of the academies to direct traffic through the unknown exposed them to charges of unenlightened despotism, while new scientific fantasies appeared faster than they could build detours around the old. "Never have so many systems, so many new theories of the universe, appeared as during the last few years," the *Journal de Physique* remarked wearily in December 1781, adding that they were mutually contradictory.[8]

8. Article "chimie" by G.-F. Venel in the *Encyclopédie, ou Dictionnaire raisonné des sciences, des arts et des métiers,* 1 ed. (Paris, 1751–1780), III, 409–410; *Journal de Physique,* December 1781, p. 503. In *The Edge of Objectivity: An Essay in the History of Scientific Ideas* (Princeton, 1960), p. 184, C. C. Gillispie cites Venel's article as an example of a "romantic" reaction among eighteenth-century scientists, especially biologists, to the rational, mathematical physics of the seventeenth century.

A glance at the scientific periodicals of the time shows the profusion of cosmologies at a popular level. One man claims to have explained the secret of life by a vitalistic "vegetative force"; a second, announcing a new kind of motionless astronomy, says he has found "the key to all the sciences, which the finest minds of all nations have sought in vain for such a long time"; a third fills Newton's void with an invisible "universal agent," which holds the cosmos together; a fourth overturns the "idol" of gravity by explaining that Newton got it backward—combustion from the sun really repels the planets; and as for Newton's ether, an electrified, "animal" version of it courses through our bodies, determining the color of our skin, according to a fifth. Even literary periodicals mixed science and fiction. The *Année littéraire*, for example, published an attack on mesmerism that was based on a rival theory of "igneous atoms," "universal fluid," and the following physiology: "In man and animals, lungs are an electric machine, which, by their continual movement, separate air from fire; the latter insinuates itself in the blood and moves by this means to the brain, which distributes it, impels it and forms it into animal spirits, which circulate in the nerves, providing all voluntary and involuntary movement."[9] These ideas did not spring from sheer fancy; they were related to those of Stahl, Boerhaave, and even Lavoisier.

The barrage of theories naturally left the reading public confused—confused, but not discouraged, for these invisible forces sometimes performed miracles. One of those gases carried Pilâtre de Rozier into the air over Metz on October 15, 1783, and the news of man's first flight struck the imaginations of Frenchmen in a wave of enthusiasm for science. Women wore "chapeaux au ballon," children ate "dragées au ballon," poets com-

9. *Mercure de France,* January 24, 1784, p. 166, and November 20, 1784, p. 142; *Journal de Physique,* September 1781, pp. 247–248, October 1781, p. 268 (continuing an article in the September issue, pp. 192–199), and September 1781, p. 176; *Année littéraire,* I (1785), 279–280.

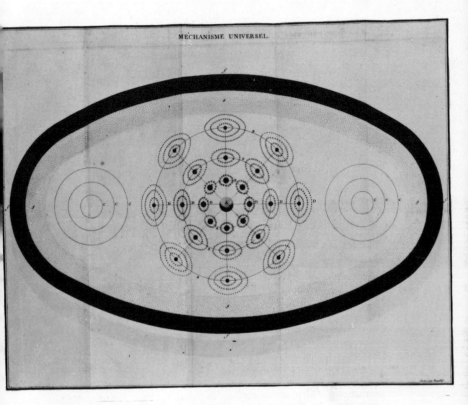

A typical cosmology, as illustrated at the end of J.-L. Carra, *Nouveaux principes de physique* (Paris, 1781), vol. I. A key to the illustration explained Carra's fantasy as follows: "A. center of this universe, great pendulum of the universal mechanism; B.B.B. parallel zones; C.C.C. collateral zones; D.D.D. general systems, composed of a great number of stars or of suns; e.e.e. exatoms [gigantic celestial bodies] governing the general systems; f.f.f.f. envelope of this universe; g.g.g.g. surrounding chaos." The diagonal of *e*'s, which is difficult to identify, runs from upper left to lower right.

posed countless odes to balloon flights, engineers wrote dozens of treatises on the construction and direction of balloons for prizes sponsored by the Academy of Sciences. Heroes ventured into balloons in towns throughout the country, and admirers recorded the smallest details of their flights, for these were great moments in history. The returning "aéronautes" were paraded through towns. Boys fought to hold the bridles of their horses; workmen kissed their clothing; and their portraits, with appropriate laudatory verse, were printed and sold in the streets. Judging from contemporary accounts of their trips, one feels the enthusiasm must have equaled at least the excitement over Lindberg's flight and the first ventures into space: "It is impossible to describe that moment: the women in tears, the common people raising their hands toward the sky in deep silence; the passengers, leaning out of the gallery, waving and crying out in joy . . . you follow them with your eyes, you call to them as if they could hear, and the feeling of fright gives way to one of wonder. No one said anything but, 'Great God, how beautiful!' Grand military music began to play and firecrackers proclaimed their glory."[10]

10. *Journal de Bruxelles*, January 31, 1784, pp. 226–227. Almost all journals of 1784 printed similar descriptions of the flights, including many rapturous accounts by the balloonists of the sensations of flying and of man's first bird's-eye-views of towns and countryside. Pilâtre de Rozier's report, published in *Journal de Bruxelles*, July 31, 1784, pp. 223–229, is a good example.

A balloon flight at Lyons in January 1784. The poem expresses the widespread conviction that science had made man almost a god, because it demonstrated the ability of his reason to under- stand and to command the laws of nature. The last line reads, "And the feeble mortal can approach the gods."

Aerostatic experiment made at Lyons in January 1784 with a balloon 100 feet in diameter. View from the southern Pavillon of Sr. Antonio Spréafico, aux Brotteaux. An infinite space separated us from the skies;/But, thanks to the Montgolfiers, whom genius inspires,/The eagle of Jupiter has lost his empire,/And the feeble mortal can ap- proach the gods.

EXPÉRIENCE AÉROSTATIQUE.

Faite à Lyon en Janvier 1784. avec un Ballon de 100 pieds de diamètre.

Vuë prise du Pavillon méridional de St Antonio Spréafico, aux Brotteaux,

Un espace infini nous séparoit des Cieux ;

Mais, Grace aux Montgolfier, que le génie inspire,

L'Aigle de Jupiter à perdu son Empire,

Et le faible mortel peut s'approcher des Dieux.

A Paris chez Crepy rue S. Jacques à S. Pierre près la rue de la parcheminerie.

The enthusiasm for balloon flights drove home the importance of science for ordinary Frenchmen in a way that Lavoisier's reports to the Academy of Sciences could never have done. One hundred thousand weeping, cheering, fainting spectators reportedly watched a flight at Nantes. When a flight at Bordeaux was canceled, the crowd rioted, killing two men and destroying the balloon and the ticket house. "They were laborers who were angry at having lost a day's work without having seen anything," the *Journal de Bruxelles* explained. Thus the flights reached audiences full of men who could not read the *Journal de Physique*. A group of peasants, for example, reportedly greeted a balloon landing in a field by shouting, "Are you men or gods?" And at the other extreme of French society, a well-born balloon enthusiast imagined seeing "the gods of antiquity carried on clouds; myths have come to life in the marvels of physics." Science had made man a god. The scientist's ability to harness the forces of nature had inspired the French with awe, with an almost religious enthusiasm, which spread beyond the scientific bodies of Paris, beyond the limits of literacy, and, as far as literary matters went, beyond the boundaries of prose. Thus one of the dozens of poems, inspired by the balloon flights, on the nobility of man's reason:

> *Tes tubes ont de l'air détérminé le poids;*
> *Ton prisme a divisé les rayons de la lumière;*
> *Le feu, la terre et l'eau soumis à tes lois:*
> *Tu domptes la nature entière.*

Science had opened limitless vistas of human progress: "The incredible discoveries that have multiplied during the last ten years . . . the phenomena of electricity fathomed, the elements transformed, the airs decomposed and understood, the rays of the sun condensed, air traversed by human audacity, a thousand other phenomena have prodigiously extended the sphere of our knowledge. Who knows how far we can go? What mortal would dare set limits to the human mind . . . ?"[11]

It seems safe, therefore, to draw one conclusion from the pulp literature of the 1780's: the reading public of that era was intoxicated with the power of science, and it was bewildered by the real and imaginary forces with which scientists peopled the universe. Because the public could not distinguish the real from the imaginary, it seized on any invisible fluid, any scientific-sounding hypothesis, that promised to explain the wonders of nature.

A hoax about the invention of "elastic shoes" laid bare these attitudes in 1783. On December 8, the *Journal de Paris* printed a letter from a watchmaker, "D . . . ," announcing the discovery of a new principle, based on ricochets, that would enable man to walk on water. D . . . promised to walk across the Seine on New Year's Day in a special pair of shoes he had invented, if a subscription of 200 louis were to await his arrival near the Pont Neuf. Within a week the journal had collected 3,243 livres from some of the most prominent men in the country, including Lafayette, who gave one of the largest contributions. The burst of enthusiasm for the project, the imposing names on the list of subscribers, and the

11. *Journal de Bruxelles,* May 29, 1784, pp. 226–227 (on the Bordeaux riot, see also *Courier de l'Europe* [London], May 28, 1784, p. 340; and July 20, 1784, p. 43, for a report of a similar riot in Paris); *Courier de l'Europe,* August 24, 1784, p. 128; *Le Journal des Sçavans,* January 1784, p. 27; *Almanach des Muses* (Paris, 1785), p. 51; *Traces du magnétisme* (The Hague, 1784), p. 4. The poem from the *Almanach des Muses* may be translated literally as follows: "Your tubes have determined the weight of the air;/Your prism has divided the rays of light;/Fire, earth and water subject to your laws:/You dominate all of nature." The *Courier de l'Europe,* July 9, 1784, p. 23, described the flight of the balloon Le Suffrein from Nantes as follows: "Cent mille âmes, au moins, assistèrent au départ du Suffrein: plusieurs femmes s'évanouirent, d'autres fondaient en larmes; tout le monde était dans une agitation inexprimable. Le retour de ces deux voyageurs . . . fut célébré comme un jour de triomphe . . . les routes étaient bordées de monde . . . la plupart des maisons illuminées. Les gens du peuple baisaient leurs mains, leurs habits . . ."

lack of precautions taken by the journal pointed to the same attitude. Man had just conquered the air; why could he not walk on water? What limits could be set to the invisible powers at the command of his reason? The hoax was exposed by the end of December. The journal converted the funds into a charity drive, and by February 7 it had overcome its embarrassment well enough to print a letter promoting a technique for seeing in the dark, which was sponsored by a club of balloon enthusiasts convinced of the brotherhood of "nyctalopes, hydrophobes, somnambulists and water witchers."[12]

L.-S. Mercier described the spirit of his contemporaries with his usual insight while reporting a subscription for a new kind of flying machine. "Love of the marvelous always conquers us, because, sensing confusedly how little we know of the forces of nature, we ecstatically welcome anything that leads us to discoveries about them." He found that Parisians' passion for science had overcome their old interest in letters, and J.-H. Meister, another perceptive commentator on Parisian fashions, concurred. "In all of our gatherings, at all our suppers, at the toilettes of our lovely women as in our academic lyceums, we talk of nothing but experiments, atmospheric air, inflammable gas, flying chariots, journeys in the air." Parisians flocked to public lecture courses on science, which were advertised in the newspapers, and scrambled for membership in the scientific lyceums and museums established by Pilâtre de Rozier, Condorcet, Court de Gébelin, and La Blancherie. The excitement that animated these adult education courses can be judged from a letter from a provincial gentleman to his friends at home on the latest vogues in Paris (see Appendix II); and the tone of the lectures can be appreciated from an article in a journal published by the Museum of La

---

12. *Journal de Paris,* December 8–26, 1783, pp. 1403–1484, and February 7, 1784, pp. 169–170.

VUE DU TRAJET DE LA RIVIERE DE SEINE À PIED SEC,
au deſſous du Pont neuf au moyen des SABOTS elaſtiques.
Dedié aux Souscripteurs.

Gravé d'après le Deſſin du Redacteur du Journal
de Paris Janv.^r 1784.

De la part de M. de Combles
Magistrat de Lyon, Inventeur.

An artist's version of the "elastic shoes" experiment. Like most
hoaxes, the experiment laid bare contemporary attitudes in
this case, the belief that scientific progress meant that man could
do anything—fly, walk on water, cure all disease.

*View of the crossing of the river Seine on dry feet beneath the Pont
Neuf by means of elastic shoes. Dedicated to the subscribers.*

Blancherie: "Ever since a predilection for science began to spread among us, we have seen the public occupied successively with physics, natural history, and chemistry; seen it not only concerned with their progress, but actually devoted to their study; the public swarms into courses where they are taught, it rushes to read books about them, and it welcomes avidly everything that brings them to mind; there are but few rich persons in whose homes one cannot find the instruments suitable for these useful sciences."[13]

The enthusiasm of amateur scientists permeated the periodicals of the 1780's and warmed the hearts of dedicated experimenters like Joseph Priestley, who observed that electrical demonstrations had become enormously fashionable and who then fed the fashion by publishing dozens of do-it-yourself experiments, designed purely for entertainment. Priestley's less eminent French counterpart, the Abbé J. A. Nollet, who championed a theory of electricity that somewhat resembled Mesmer's fluid, wrote several such manuals for amateurs, and publications like the *Journal de Physique* reviewed many similar works aimed at what must have been an extensive readership of home scientists. Amateurs playing with sulphur and electricity could hope to stumble upon some discovery like the one announced in the *Journal de Paris* of May 11, 1784, by J.-L. Carra, the future Girondist leader. Journals snatched at such reports from their readers "especially these days, when one searches eagerly for everything

13. L.-S. Mercier, *Tableau de Paris,* 12 vols. (Amsterdam, 1782–1788), II, 300; also XI, 18: "Le règne des lettres est passé; les physiciens remplacent les poètes et les romanciers; la machine électrique tient lieu d'une pièce de théâtre." Meister's remark is in *Correspondance littéraire, philosophique et critique par Grimm, Diderot, Raynal, Meister, etc.,* ed. Maurice Tourneux (Paris, 1880), XIII, 344 (cited henceforth as Grimm's *Correspondance littéraire*). The account of La Blancherie's Musée is in *Nouvelles de la République des lettres,* October 12, 1785. The enthusiasm for the lycées and musées of Paris can be documented from numerous articles in *Mémoires secrets pour servir à l'histoire de la république des lettres en France,* as well as other publications.

connected with some discovery," as the *Journal de Bruxelles* put it. As if to illustrate its remark, the journal published excited accounts of discoveries like the "styptic water" that, according to the habitués of the Café du Caveau of Paris, stopped all hemorrhages. Not to be outdone by its competitor, the *Courier de l'Europe* published a report of a Parisian who claimed to cure all ills with a mixture of bread and opium, a prescription that held out hope for the readers of the *Journal de Physique,* who had been warned that their cooking utensils were probably poisonous. Judging from their letters-to-the-editor, the readers of these periodicals believed science could do anything. A certain M. d'Audouard of Marseilles notified the *Courier de l'Europe* of the invention of a perpetual motion machine that would grind grain on its own power forever, and a seven-year-old boy who had confided his bed-wetting problems to the *Journal de Paris* was advised to give himself periodic electric shocks. An old-fashioned literary type complained to the *Année littéraire* that "this scientific mania" had gone too far. "For literature one has but a cold esteem bordering on indifference, while the sciences . . . excite a universal enthusiasm. Physics, chemistry, natural history have become a craze."[14]

Amateur science provided amusement, if nothing else. Scientist-magicians like Joseph Pinetti toured the country performing "amusing physics and various

14. Priestley, *The History and Present State of Electricity,* II, 134–138, and *passim; Journal de Bruxelles,* January 10, 1784, p. 81, and March 6, 1784, p. 39 (see also May 15, 1784, p. 139); *Courier de l'Europe,* October 8, 1784, p. 228; *Journal de Physique,* July 1781, p. 80; *Courier de l'Europe,* August 27, 1784, p. 135; *Journal de Paris,* April 23, 1784, p. 501, and April 27, 1784, pp. 516–517; *Année littéraire* I (1785), 5, 8. Mallet du Pan put mesmerism in its proper context while reporting on its enormous popularity in his *Journal historique et politique* (Geneva), February 14, 1784, p. 321: "Les arts, les sciences, tout fourmille aujourd'hui d'inventions, de prodiges, de talents surnaturels. Une foule de gens de tout état, qui ne s'étaient jamais douté d'être chimistes, géomètres, mécaniciens etc. etc. etc. se présentent journellement avec des merveilles de toute espèce."

entertaining experiments." A certain M. de Kempelen delighted Parisians in the summer of 1784 by exhibiting his scientific wonder, the chess-playing robot. The "têtes parlantes" (talking heads) of the Abbé Mical elicited a serious investigation by the Academy of Sciences and a rapturous letter in the *Mercure* by Mallet du Pan about the new science of creating speech, the "thousand marvels" of science in general, and Parisians' "general frenzy about experiments regarded as supernatural." Henri Decremps, who called himself a "professor and demonstrator of amusing physics," capitalized on this attitude in a series of popular scientific books that were, in effect, manuals for magicians. He treated dozens of tricks like the dancing egg that jumps out of a hat and the mechanical singing bird as "a simple problem of physics or mathematics" and analyzed the current scientific fads just as Priestley and Lavoisier had done: "When visible, striking phenomena depend upon an imperceptible and unknown cause, the human mind, ever inclined toward the marvelous, naturally attributes these effects to a chimerical cause." The popular faith in scientific marvels also expressed itself in plays like *L'Amour physicien,* performed at the Ambigu-Comique on January 1, 1784, and *Le ballon ou la Physico-manie,* which opened at the Variétés Amusantes later that year, and even in science fiction novels like *Aventures singulières d'un voyageur aërien; Le retour de mon pauvre oncle, ou relation de son voyage dans la lune; Baby-Bambon, histoire archimerveilleuse;* and *Nouvelles du monde lunaire.* The fiction may not have seemed too extravagant, for Pilâtre de Rozier had boasted that he could fly in his balloon from Calais to Boston in two days, if the winds were right. Popular science even found its way into love letters, at least in the case of Linguet's mistress, who asked him not to send her light verse, "because I only like poems when they are dressed up in a bit of physics or metaphysics." A kindred spirit, the future Girondist leader C. J. M. Barbaroux, found that only poetry could express the excitement of his experiments with electricity:

> O feu subtil, âme du monde,
> Bienfaisante électricité
> Tu remplis l'air, la terre, l'onde,
> Le ciel et son immensité.[15]

This was the spirit of the time in which Condorcet, then secretary of the Academy of Sciences, nurtured his vision of human progress. The reports of experiments, gadgets, and scientific debates crammed into publications ranging from the cautious *Journal de Paris* to the clandestine *bulletins à la main* give the impression that the golden age of popular science occurred in prerevolutionary France, rather than in nineteenth- or twentieth-century America.

So strong was the popular enthusiasm for science in the 1780's that it almost erased the line (never very clear until the nineteenth century) dividing science from pseudoscience. The government and the learned societies, which attempted to hold that line against the incursions

15. *Mercure*, July 3, 1784, p. 45, and July 24, 1784, p. 177; Henri Decremps, *La magie blanche dévoilée, ou explication des tours surprenants, qui font depuis peu l'admiration de la capitale et de la province, avec des réflexions sur la baguette divinatoire, les automates joueurs d'échecs etc. etc.* (Paris, 1784), pp. xi, 72. The letter to Linguet is cited in Jean Cruppi, *Un avocat journaliste au XVIIIe siècle: Linguet* (Paris, 1895), p. 307. Barbaroux's poem is in *Mémoires inédits de Pétion et mémoires de Buzot & de Barbaroux . . .* ed. C. A. Dauban (Paris, 1866), p. 264. Translated literally, it goes: "Oh subtle fire, soul of the world,/Beneficent electricity/You fill the air, the earth, the sea,/The sky and its immensity." See also Decremps' *Supplément à la Magie blanche dévoilée* (Paris, 1785), pp. 281–282, which described the character of the modern charlatan: "Il se vante ordinairement d'avoir découvert de nouvelles lois dans la nature inconnues jusqu'à lui; mais il s'en réserve toujours le secret, en assurant que ses connaissances sont du ressort de la physique occulte . . . Il prétend d'être plus éclairé que toutes les sociétés savantes." Decremps pursued his attacks on popular "magic" scientists in *Testament de Jerome Sharp, professeur de physique amusante* (Paris, 1789) and *Codicile de Jerome Sharp* (Paris, 1791).

of quacks and charlatans, condemned Mesmer but gave their blessing to Nicolas le Dru, a sort of vaudevillian from the Foire Saint-Germain, who propounded a theory of a universal fluid like Mesmer's and established a magnetic treatment for the sick in the Couvent des Célestins. Imposing apparatus and theories inspired faith in several projects like the elastic shoes. A certain Bottineau, for

A monster believed to have been captured in South America. This cartoon and others like it were sold widely in the streets of Paris. The reports of monsters were taken seriously by some newspapers and did not seem too absurd in the light of eighteenth-century theories of sexual generation and the cross-breeding of species.

Description of this unique monster seizing its prey. This monster was found in the kingdom of Santa Fe, Peru, in the province of Chili and in the Lake of Fagua, located in the lands of Prosper Voston. It emerged during the night in order to devour the swine, cows, and bulls of the area. Its length is eleven feet; its face is roughly that of a man; its mouth is as wide as its face; it is provided with teeth two inches long; it has twenty-four-inch horns like those of a bull; its hair reaches to the ground; it has four-inch ears like those of an ass; it has two bat-like wings; its thighs and legs are twenty-five inches long and its claws eight; it has two tails, one very flexible and provided with rings that help it seize its prey, and the other ending in a dart, which helps it kill; its entire body is covered with scales. This monster was captured by many men who had laid traps into which it fell. It was entangled in nets and brought alive to the viceroy, who succeeded in nourishing it with a steer, a cow, or a bull, given to it every day with three or four swine, to which it is quite partial. As it would be necessary to load too great a quantity of cattle to nourish it during the crossing, which takes at least five or six months to pass Cape Horn, the viceroy has sent orders along the entire land route to provide for the needs of this unique monster while making it march by stages to the Gulf of Honduras, where it will embark for Havana. From there to the Bermudas, to the Azores, and in three weeks it will disembark at Cadiz. From Cadiz it will be taken by short trips to the royal family. It is hoped that the female will be captured so that the species will not die out in Europe. The species seems to be that of harpies, heretofore considered legendary.

example, developed a technique for perceiving ships in a fog, and a peasant from the Dauphiny called Bléton was said to have entertained about 30,000 persons with the spectacular feats of his water-witching "experiments" in 1781 and 1782. The discovery by a M. de la Taupinardière of a method of breathing and traveling underground (he promised to burrow under the bridge of Avignon on January 1, 1784) was spotted by the *Courier de l'Europe* as an obvious hoax, but the *Courier* hailed the capture of a Chilean monster (man's face, lion's mane,

Description de ce Monstre unique se saisissant de sa Proye;

snake's scales, bull's horns, bat's wings, two tails) as "a beautiful opportunity . . . for the naturalists of the New and Old Worlds." Engravings of the monster circulated in Paris, making it the subject of "all the talk" for a week, and prompting the *Courier* to reflect solemnly that it proved the truth of ancient fables about harpies and sirens. This was no absurd opinion at a time when ovists, animalculists, preformationists, and panspermatists outdid each other in speculation about sexual generation; when Restif de la Bretonne and, evidently, Mirabeau believed that Frederick II had produced centaurs and satyrs by experiments with sodomy; and when Jacques-Pierre Brissot feared that sodomy would disfigure the human race, noting that "everyone has heard of the child-calf and the child-wolf."[16]

"Everyone" certainly had heard of the extravagant machines that showed the gadgeteering side of the boundless faith in science. The *Journal de Bruxelles* applauded the invention of an "hydrostatergatic" machine for traveling underwater but raised doubts about the canvas wings and tail with which a man proposed to fly in Provence: "These experiments have gone to the heads of the weak-minded to such an extent that hardly a day goes by without some more or less extravagant project being named and believed." A. J. Renaux sized up the mood of his contemporaries in a prospectus he circulated in Paris. He asked only for a subscription of 24,000 livres and a lodging in the Ecole Militaire in return for developing a machine that would fly (without gas or smoke),

16. *Mémoires secrets,* November 27, 1783, pp. 54–55, December 6, 1783, pp. 74–75, and April 9, 1784, p. 255; Grimm's *Correspondance littéraire,* XIII, 387–388; Pierre Thouvenel, *Mémoire physique et médicinal montrant des rapports évidents entre les phénomènes de la baguette divinatoire, du magnétisme et de l'électricité* (London, 1781), and its sequel, *Second mémoire physique et médicinal . . .* (London, 1784); *Courier de l'Europe,* January 9, 1784, p. 18, October 22, 1784, p. 260, and October 29, 1784, p. 276; Restif de la Bretonne, *Monsieur Nicolas ou le coeur humain dévoilé* (Paris, 1959), V, 530; J.-P. Brissot, *Théorie des loix criminelles* (Berlin, 1781), I, 243.

hoist heavy weights, pump water, grind grain, and travel on rivers. Moreover he promised new methods of heating and cooling apartments, salvaging sunken ships, communicating thoughts with great speed over great distances, and seeing objects on other planets as clearly as if they were on earth.[17]

Pseudoscience, in turn, carried Parisians into the territory of occultism, which had bordered on science since the Middle Ages. Cagliostro was only the most famous of the many alchemists Mercier found in Paris. Street venders hawked engravings of the Comte de Saint Germain, "célèbre alchimiste," and booksellers displayed alchemist works like *Discours philosophiques sur les trois principes animal, végétal & minéral; ou la suite de la clef qui ouvre les portes du sanctuaire philosophique* by Claude Chevalier. Unable to afford proper doctors, the poor turned, as always, to the cheaper exploitation of the quacks and faithhealers in the underworld of medicine— and probably fared better for it. "Secret remedies of all kinds are distributed daily, despite the rigor of the prohibitions," the *Mercure* noted. Such practices probably had always existed, but in July 1784 a Parisian correspondent of the *Journal de Bruxelles* remarked on the era's peculiar plethora of "hermetic, cabalistic, and theosophic philosophers, propagating fanatically all the old absurdities of theurgy, of divination, of astrology etc." In the periodicals of the time, one often meets characters like Léon le Juif, who performed miracles with mirrors; Ruer, who possessed the philosopher's stone; B. J. Labre de Damette, the beggar-healer; and unidentifiable others— St. Hubert, the genie Alael, the "prophète de la rue des Moineaux," the faith-healer of the rue des Ciseaux, the "toucheur" who cured by mystic signs and touches, the purveyors of an all-curative "sympathetic powder" invented by Sir Kenelm Digby in the seventeenth century,

17. *Journal de Bruxelles,* February 14, 1784, pp. 85–87, and August 7, 1784, p. 38; *Journal des Sçavans,* September 1784, pp. 627–629.

and the child who could see underground. Even serious scientists had long been publishing accounts in the *Journal des Sçavans* and the *Journal de Physique* of marvels like talking dogs and basilisks whose looks killed quicker than bullets. To maintain that certain fountains dried up when impure women bathed in them was to demonstrate common sense in a day when the heritage of alchemy, with its myths about magic potions that caused immortality and cured all diseases, could not easily be dismissed as nonsense. Alchemists, sorcerers, and fortune tellers had imbedded themselves so deeply in Parisian life that the police found them to be better even than priests at spying and providing secret information. Honest spiritualists like L.-C. de Saint-Martin, J.-B. Willermoz, and J.-C. Lavater also flourished. They were cited in mesmerist works and practiced mesmerism themselves. Spiritualism seemed to complement the efforts of scientists like Goethe and Goethe's Faust to penetrate the vitalistic forces in the very marrow of the matter that

A typical plan for flying machines. It illustrates the gadgeteering aspect of the enthusiasm for popular science and shows the ancestry of modern fantasies about travel through space. The "aeronauts" have left their airships and are landing by means of their "aerostatic clothes," which also help them to navigate in water.

The two balloons, full of inflammable air, follow a set direction, while the third, destitute of its gas and sustained by the immense surface it exposes to the air, is directed with the help of a rudder to a favorable place. The two travelers who float in the air with aerostatic costumes and "manivoles" in their hands have left that vessel, as has the traveler on the ground. He has his costume tucked up and his "manivoles" near him. They all have cork jackets to help them skim along the water. A compass on the front of the jackets is intended to guide the travelers when fog or distance prevent them from seeing earth. The sort of crow's nest on top of the balloons is to hold a man who could help in maneuvering the sails.

EXPLICATION.

Les deux Ballons, pleins d'air inflamable, suivent une direction déterminée, tandis que le troisieme dépourvu de son Gaz, et soutenu par l'immence surface qu'il présente à l'air, se dirige à l'aide de son gouvernail, vers un lieu propice; les deux Voyageurs qui planent en l'air, avec des habits Aérostatiques et des Manivoles en mains, ont quitté ce Bâtiment, ainsi que le Voyageur qui est à terre; celui-ci a son habit retroussé et ses manivoles près de lui. tous ont des Scaphandres, pour les faciliter à voguer sur l'eau; une Boussole qui est sur le devant de ces Scaphandres, a pour objet de guider les Voyageurs, lors que les Brouillards ou l'éloignement leurs empêchervient de voir la terre; l'espece de Lenterne, qui est en haut des Ballons, doit contenir un homme pour faciliter la manœuvre des voiles.

Nil tam difficile est, quin quærundo investigari poßiet. *Terent in Hoant.*

Paris chez M. Fessard, Rue Amelot même Maison de M. Berger Salpetrier du Roi, au Pont aux Choux.

A. P. D. R.

Thb. St André in et del.   M. Fessard, Sculp.

earlier scientists had only weighed and measured out-
wardly. Mesmerism seemed to be a spiritualist science;
in fact some mesmerists described it as a modern, scientific version of the mystic strain in Jansenism: the convulsionaries had suffered mesmeric crises and ". . . the tomb
of Saint Médard was a mesmeric tub." Jean-Jacques Duval
d'Eprémesnil, leader of the resistance to the government
by the once heavily Jansenist Parlement of Paris, combined his mesmerizing with support of Cagliostro, Saint-
Martin, and Dr. James Graham.[18]

Thus mesmerism seems to have occupied a place
somewhere near the middle of the spectrum in which

18. The quotations come from the *Mercure,* March 13, 1784, p. 94,
and April 17, 1784, p. 113; *Journal de Bruxelles,* July 24, 1784, p. 171;
and Galart de Montjoie, *Lettres sur le magnétisme animal, où l'on examine
la conformité des opinions des peuples anciens & modernes, des sçavans &
notamment de M. Bailly avec celles de M. Mesmer . . .* (Philadelphia, 1784),
p. 10. On these and other forms of occultism, see: *Mémoires secrets,*
August 11, 1783, pp. 113–116; Mercier, *Tableau de Paris,* II, 299–300,
VIII, 176, 299, 341, IX, 25, XI, 291–293, 352–355; Grimm's *Correspondance
littéraire,* XIII, 387–388; *Mesmer justifié* (Constance, 1784), p. 34; *Remarques
sur la conduite du sieur Mesmer, de son commis le P. Hervier et de ses adhérents* (1784), p. 26; *Eclaircissemens sur le magnétisme animal* (London, 1784),
pp. 6–8; *L'Antimagnétisme . . .* (London, 1784), p. 3; the memoirs of Duclos
in *Bibliothèque des mémoires relatifs à l'histoire de France pendant le 18e
siècle, nouvelle série* (Paris, 1880–1881), XXVII, 20; and *Avertissement de
M. D'Eprémesnil, à l'occasion de quelques écrits anonymes qu'il a reçus
de Beaucaire par la poste* (1789). For a description of a typical alchemist
session of the 1780's, see R. M. Le Suire (pseudonym), *Le Philosophe
parvenu . . .* (London, 1787), I, 204–211. On the police and spiritualism,
see *Mémoires tirés des archives de la police de Paris . . .* ed. J. Peuchet
(Paris, 1838), III, 98, 102–103. The indispensable general study of this
obscure subject is Auguste Viatte, *Les sources occultes du romantisme,
illuminisme-théosophie 1770–1820,* 2 vols. (Paris, 1928).

A satirical picture of the fashionable, foppish sort of amateur
scientist. This "physicist" plans to escape his creditors and his
mistresses by flying away in a balloon outfit.

*The little-master physicist. On earth I am overcome/Both by debts
and by caresses./I flee in the air, it's decided:/Good-bye creditors
and mistresses.*

LE PETIT-MAITRÉ PHYSICIEN

Sur Terre je suis excédé   *Je suis dans l'Air c'est décidé.*
Et de dettes et de caresses.   *Adieu Créanciers et Maitresses.*

science shaded off into pseudoscience and occultism. By 1788, Mercier himself, whose *Tableau de Paris* reflected most nuances of opinion in prerevolutionary Paris, had moved beyond mesmerism to the belief of a "new sect" that the world was full of invisible ghosts. "We are in an unknown world," he explained. Such beliefs did not mark one as an eccentric in those days; they were the height of fashion. For example, a play, *Les illuminés,* featured Cléante, "a fashionable young man and an illuminist" (un jeune homme à la mode et illuminé), dominating a debate in a stylish salon. Cléante adopted "that sentimental language that makes us transmit our thoughts from one pole to the other" in order to communicate with ghosts and to defend mesmerism. "Nothing is more luminous: it is the true system of the universe, the mover of all things." The Cléantes of Paris did not consider such romantic gushing unscientific; they felt that it was the proper style of science and of occultism or what they called "high science" (haute science). Even the most occult of Mesmer's followers rejected any suggestion that they were repudiating the scientific advances of their century. Court de Gébelin, the highly esteemed author of *Le Monde Primitif,* described mesmerism and "the supernatural sciences" as the natural products of recent scientific discoveries. One of his fellow mesmerists exulted that "physics would take the place of magic everywhere"; and another explained, "Above science is magic, because magic follows it, not as an effect, but as its perfection." The similarity between Mesmer's ideas and some respectable fantasies of the academicians who attacked them strengthened this argument. J. S. Bailly, the author of the royal commission's report condemning mesmerism, held scientific theories that, as mesmerist pamphlets noted, embarrassingly resembled Mesmer's, and readers might even confuse the description of caloric by Lavoisier, another member of the commission, with Mesmer's account of his fluid. In short, mesmerism suited the interest in science and "high science" during the decade before the Revolution, and it did not seem to contradict the spirit of the Enlightenment. A contemporary mesmerist list of authors whose works "have some analogy with mesmerism" went as follows: "Locke, Bacon, Bayle, Leibniz, Hume, Newton, Descartes, La Mettrie, Bonnet, Diderot, Maupertuis, Robinet, Helvétius, Condillac, J.-J. Rousseau, Buffon, Marat, Bertholon." In its first stages, mesmerism expressed the Enlightenment's faith in reason taken to an extreme, an Enlightenment run wild, which later was to provoke a movement toward the opposite extreme in the form of romanticism. Mesmerism played a role in this movement, too: it showed the point at which the two extremes met. But it had not reached this point in the mid-1780's, when a wit put it neatly in perspective:

> Autrefois Moliniste
> Ensuite Janséniste
> Puis Encyclopédiste
> Et puis Economiste
> A présent Mesmériste . . .[19]

19. Mercier, *Tableau de Paris*, XII, 352–355; *Les illuminés* in *Le Somnambule* . . . (1786), by Fanny de Beauharnais, according to A. A. Barbier (Alexis Dureau is certainly wrong in attributing it to Pierre Didot, who, as a member of the Society of Harmony, would not have satirized mesmerism); Court de Gébelin, *Lettre de l'auteur du Monde Primitif à Messieurs ses souscripteurs sur le magnétisme animal* (Paris, 1784), pp. 16–18; Thouvenel, *Mémoire physique et médicinal*, p. 31; *Fragment sur les hautes sciences* . . . (Amsterdam, 1785), p. 10. Galart de Montjoie exposed the parallels between the ideas of Bailly and Gébelin in *Lettres sur le magnétisme animal*. On Lavoisier's caloric, see his description of it in *Traité élémentaire de chimie*, I, 4 ("un fluide très-subtil qui s'insinue à travers les molécules de tous les corps et qui les écarte"), and Maurice Daumas, *Lavoisier, théoricien et expérimentateur* (Paris, 1955), pp. 162–171. The mesmerist list of philosophes is in *Appel au public sur le magnétisme animal* . . . (1787), p. 49. The epigram, from the *Mémoires secrets*, May 25, 1784, p. 11, may be translated: "Formerly Molinist/Later Jansenist/Then Encyclopedist/And then Economist/At present Mesmerist . . ."

Mesmerism corresponded so well to the attitudes of literate Frenchmen that it probably inspired more interest than any other topic or fashion during the decade before the edict of July 5, 1788, concerning the convocation of the Estates General, initiated a free-for-all of political pamphleteering. Although it is difficult to measure this interest with any precision, it certainly varied, mounting steadily from 1779 to 1784 and declining after 1785; and contemporary accounts indicate unmistakably that, as La Harpe put it, mesmerism prevailed as "an epidemic that has overcome all of France." Mesmerism occupied more space by far than any other topic in the *Mémoires secrets* and the *Journal de Paris* for 1783–1784, the time of its greatest vogue. Even the *Almanach des Muses* for 1785 is full of poems (mostly hostile) about it. The bookseller S. P. Hardy noted in his private journal that the "frenzy" of mesmerism had overcome even the passion for balloon flights. "Men, women, children, everyone is involved, everyone mesmerizes," remarked the *Mémoires secrets;* and Meister concurred: "Everyone is occupied with mesmerism. One is dazzled with its marvels, and if one admits doubts about its powers . . . at least one dares no longer deny its existence." "The great subject of all conversations in the capital is still animal magnetism," said the *Courier de l'Europe;* and the *Journal de Bruxelles* reported, "We are concerned only with animal magnetism . . ."[20] Mesmerism was debated in the academies, salons, and cafés. It was investigated by the police, patronized by the queen, ridiculed several times on the stage, burlesqued in popular songs, doggerels, and cartoons, practiced in a network of masonic-like secret

20. J.-F. La Harpe, *Correspondance littéraire* . . . (Paris, 1801–1807), IV, 266; Hardy's manuscript journal, Bibliothèque Nationale, fonds français, 6684, May 1, 1784, p. 444 (Hardy paid much less attention to mesmerism than did most *nouvellistes); Mémoires secrets,* April 9, 1784, p. 254; Grimm's *Correspondance littéraire,* XIII, 510; *Courier de l'Europe,* October 5, 1784, p. 219; *Journal de Bruxelles,* May 22, 1784, p. 179.

societies, and publicized by a flood of pamphlets and books. It even found its way into *Così fan tutte,* by Mesmer's friend from his days in Vienna, Wolfgang Amadeus Mozart.

The enormous interest in mesmerism provides some clues to the mentality of literate Frenchmen on the eve of the Revolution. In the pamphlet literature during the decade before the calling of the Estates General one rarely meets any sophisticated political ideas or analysis of key issues like the land tax. French pamphleteers produced at least twice as many works on mesmerism as on the six-month political crisis accompanying the first Assembly of Notables. Failing to foresee the Revolution, Frenchmen did not interest themselves in political theory. They discussed mesmerism and other apolitical fads, like balloon flights. Why, indeed, should they have tortured themselves with the difficult and seemingly irrelevant abstractions of the *Social Contract* when they could fill their thoughts with Chilean monsters, flying machines, and the other miracles offered them by the wonderful, invisible powers of science? True, the censorship prevented serious discussion of politics in publications like the *Journal de Paris,* France's only daily paper. True, Robespierre and other individuals took the *Social Contract* to their hearts before 1789; the American Revolution made Locke's abstractions come alive; the Académie Française had even proposed the seemingly hot topic of the abolition of serfdom for its poetry prize of 1781 and had received some rather heated entries. But the hottest topics of all, the subjects that provoked debates and aroused passions, the items with "news value" in the eyes of contemporary journalists, were mesmerism, balloon flights, and the other marvels of popular science. The *bulletins à la main,* which generally circulated independently of the censors and the police, paid relatively little attention to politics, except for great scandals like the Affair of the Diamond Necklace and spectacular events

like *lits de justice.* Politics took place in the remote world
of Versailles, often in the form of obscure intrigues around
ill-defined factions like that of the Baron de Breteuil,
the Minister of the Department of Paris, and that of
Charles-Alexandre de Calonne, the Controller-General,
and these intrigues had little relevance to the lives of
most Frenchmen before the prerevolutionary crisis of
1787–1788. In the eyes of the literate public, what was a
critical political event, like the death of the foreign
minister Vergennes, compared with the death of Pilâtre
de Rozier, the hero balloonist, after his Montgolfière-
Charlière caught fire and crashed during his attempt to
fly across the English Channel on June 15, 1785? Pilâtre's
death, not the Assembly of Notables, aroused the pamphleteering instinct in Jean-Paul Marat, who lamented,
"He [Pilâtre] was deaf to my voice, and, like another
Cassandra, I cried in the desert." Marat's pamphlet
demanded that youth study not politics but physics,
especially Marat's *Recherches physiques sur le feu* (1780)—
and two years earlier Robespierre had taken his first big
step into the public view by speaking out in defense of
lightning rods and science in general. The point may
seem labored, but it is worth emphasizing, because no
one has ever taken mesmerism and the other forms of
popular science seriously—virtually no one, that is,
since the French of the 1780's. They looked out on a
world so different from our own that we can hardly perceive it; for our view is blocked by our own cosmologies,

The death of Pilâtre de Rozier after his balloon caught fire during his attempt to cross the Channel on June 15, 1785. He had
bragged earlier that he could cross the Atlantic in two days, if
winds were favorable. The disaster checked the vogue of balloon
flights, which in its heyday had raised issues like the influence
of science on warfare, but which floundered on the more mun-
dane problem of how to guide balloons when the winds were
not favorable.

assimilated, knowingly or not, from the scientists and philosophers of the nineteenth and twentieth centuries. In the eighteenth century, the view of literate Frenchmen opened upon a splendid, baroque universe, where their gaze rode on waves of invisible fluid into realms of infinite speculation.[21]

One should not be surprised, therefore, to find radicals like Marat devoting themselves principally to fantastic treatises on light, heat, and techniques of balloon flights before 1789, nor to find that Mesmer's partisans included several important future leaders of the Revolution—Lafayette, Adrien Duport, Jacques-Pierre Brissot, Jean-Louis Carra, Nicolas Bergasse, the Rolands, and Duval d'Eprémesnil. It should help us understand the mentality of these men if we consider that on the eve of the Revolution they communicated with ghosts, with remote planets, and with one another

21. Marat's remark is in his anonymous pamphlet, *Lettres de l'observateur bon-sens à M. de xxx, sur la fatale catastrophe des infortunés Pilâtre de Rosier & Romain, les aéronautes & l'aérostation* (London, 1785), p. 19. Marat had a remote connection with Robespierre's famous lightning rod case; see A. Cabanès, *Marat inconnu: l'homme privé, le médecin, le savant,* 2 ed. (Paris, 1911), pp. 235–257. R. W. Greenlaw estimated that there were 108 political pamphlets published during the first six months of 1787 in his statistical work on this surprisingly unstudied subject, "Pamphlet Literature on the Eve of the French Revolution," *Journal of Modern History,* XXIX (1957), 354. An estimate made in 1787 put the number of mesmerist pamphlets at 200 *(Appel au public sur le magnétisme animal . . . p.* 11). This figure seems reliable, for there are 166 works in the incomplete collection of prerevolutionary mesmerist writings in the Bibliothèque Nationale. The *Mercure* of October 20, 1781, pp. 106–107, reported that the Chevalier de Langeac got an honorable mention for his poem on the abolition of serfdom, read to the Académie Française on August 25, which included denunciations of the *corvée* and *mainmorte* and lines like, "O honte! quoi, d'un Dieu les ministres sacrés/Soutiennent comme un droit ces crimes révérés!/C'est dans un siècle humain que leurs vastes domaines/S'engraissent des sueurs du Chrétien dans les chaînes!" The *Mémoires secrets* flippantly dismissed Vergennes' death (which proved a crucial factor in the government's failure to reform France peacefully in 1787) in 7 lines, and showed far more interest in Pilâtre's crash; see the entries for February 13, 1787, p. 131, and June 17 and 19, 1785, pp. 94 and 98–99.

over great distances; that they analyzed characters by the shapes of persons' faces; that they supported the claims of freakish individuals to see in the dark or to water witch; and that they performed extraordinary feats, like perceiving their own insides while in somnambulist trances and prescribing the means and date of their recovery while ill. Their thoughts drifted about among the clusters of attitudes—flighty, nebulous, and at times imperceptible to someone peering through two centuries of time—that made up the High Enlightenment. Despite its difficulties, an investigation of that remote mental universe should improve the understanding of pre-revolutionary radicalism; for radical ideas filtered down to the reading public, not as so many citations of Rousseau, but as components of contemporary interests. One may therefore turn to mesmerism, the greatest vogue of the 1780's, to see how the radical movement worked its way into the minds of ordinary literate Frenchmen.

2. THE MESMERIST MOVEMENT

The mesmerist movement ran a course of dramatic twists and turns typical of the great causes célèbres of the Ancien Régime. Its Jehovah-like founder spoke mainly through disciples like Nicolas Bergasse, who preached to the faithful for him and wrote the letters and pamphlets issued in his name. His authentic voice lies buried in history; even his contemporaries failed to understand it, for it reached them in an impenetrable German accent that made the gibberish of Cagliostro sound like clarity itself. One cannot even get close enough to the man to determine whether or not he was a charlatan; if he was, he certainly dwarfed his fellow quacks. A friend and patron of Mozart, a personage of the first order in Paris, he exerted an influence on his age that testifies to the power of the personality hidden in his robes and rituals, the power that we appropriately acknowledge in expressions such as a "mesmerized" audience or a "magnetic" personality.[1]

Mesmer was born in the village of Iznang near Constance in 1734. He studied and then practiced medicine in Vienna, where the faculty of medicine accepted the mixture of astrology and Newtonianism that he offered as his doctoral thesis, De planetarum influxu, in 1766. In 1773 he ran a magnetic clinic in company with a

1. This account of the mesmerist movement is based on: F. A. Mesmer, Mémoire sur la découverte du magnétisme animal (Geneva, 1779); Mesmer, Précis historique des faits relatifs au mangétisme animal . . . (London, 1781); Mesmer, Lettre de l'auteur de la découverte du magnétisme animal à l'auteur des Réflexions préliminaires . . . Nicolas Bergasse, Observations de M. Bergasse sur un écrit du Docteur Mesmer . . . (London, 1785); Bergasse, Supplément aux Observations . . . ; J.-J. Duval d'Eprémesnil, Sommes versées entre les mains de Monsieur Mesmer . . . ; d'Eprémesnil, Mémoire pour M. Charles-Louis Varnier . . . (Paris, 1785); F. L. T. d'Onglée, Rapport au public de quelques abus auxquels le magnétisme animal a donné lieu . . . ; and the voluminous reports in the Mémoires secrets pour servir à l'histoire de la république des lettres en France and Journal de Paris, which include letters from several leading mesmerists. The interpretation here of the general character of mesmerism is based upon a reading of the mesmerist collections in the Bibliothèque Nationale and the British Museum.

Jesuit professor of astronomy, and later, under the influence of the Swabian faith healer J. J. Gassner, found that he could cure disease by manipulating the magnetic fluid without magnets. After his practice of "animal" as opposed to "mineral" magnetism antagonized the faculty of medicine, he decided to leave for Paris, the mecca of the marvelous in eighteenth-century Europe.

Mesmer arrived in Paris in February 1778 with introductions to some well-placed persons and established his first tub in an apartment of the Place Vendôme. His imposing manner, his apparatus, and his early cures soon aroused enough attention for him to be invited to outline his theory before the Academy of Sciences. The academicians ignored him, however, and he fell back upon another tactic. He retired to the nearby village of Creteil with a group of patients he had accumulated and invited the academy to verify his cures. When the academy also snubbed this offer, he requested an investigation from the Royal Society of Medicine; but he quarreled over the verification of his patients' diseases with the commissioners sent by the society, and it refused to have any further dealings with him. Next Mesmer turned to the medical faculty of the University of Paris. His first important convert, Charles Deslon, a docteur régent of the faculty and premier médecin of the Comte d'Artois, presented him to twelve faculty doctors at a dinner party. But the doctors refused to take his Germanic metaphysics seriously and later declined even to accept a copy of his first French publication, *Mémoire sur le magnétisme animal*,

Mesmer. Translated literally, the poem goes: "A thousand jealous spirits have vainly tried to harm you,/Mesmer; by your generous care,/Our ills have disappeared, humanity respires,/Pursue your glorious destiny,/Though jealousy should grumble about it:/How beautiful, how great it is to excite envy/In producing the world's happiness."

Mille jaloux esprits en vain t'ont voulu nuire,
Mesmer, par tes soins généreux,
Nos maux ont disparus, l'humanité respire.
Poursuis tes destins glorieux
Quoique la jalousie en gronde :
Qu'il est beau, qu'il est grand d'avoir des envieux,
En faisant le bonheur du monde . .

Paris, chez Civil Graveur, rue d'Angiviler près celle des Poulies, Q.er du Louvre N.º 5.

because three faculty members had investigated his cures and attributed them to natural recoveries.

These cures, publicized by a growing number of mesmerist pamphlets, attracted ever more attention and won Mesmer a steadily increasing number of converts, including some influential persons. Mesmer's success among the fashionable amateur scientists alarmed the professionals, who by 1779 began attacking him in pamphlets and vitriolic articles in the *Journal de Médecine* and the *Gazette de Santé*. The mesmerists replied in kind, led by their master, whose *Précis historique des faits relatifs au magnétisme animal* (1781) set the tone of injured innocence and opposition to the scientific establishment that was to characterize mesmerist writing. While the violence and volume of the pamphlet war increased, the faculty resolved to extirpate the heresy by striking Deslon off its rolls. Deslon's expulsion aroused even more controversy, for the faculty, like most faculties, suffered from internal rivalries; 30 of its young doctors declared themselves partisans of the new medicine, and Deslon bravely defied the old guard by challenging them to compete with Mesmer in the treatment of 24 patients, to be chosen by lot. The conservative majority of the faculty counterattacked with a decree giving the 30 a choice of taking an oath of loyalty to orthodox medicine or being expelled. Two of the doctors followed Deslon into the freer field of popular medicine, publishing manifestos against "the most absolute despotism of opinion" of the faculty. Deslon's own expulsion, a complicated process of dramatic faculty meetings, negotiations, and legal maneuvers from September 1781 to September 1784, provided the mesmerists with a martyr whose effectiveness was spoiled only by his concurrent quarrels with Mesmer and ultimately by his death while being mesmerized in August 1786. Mesmer had his own health to worry about. He announced that he would soothe in the waters of Spa the wounds that had been inflicted on him by the academic officialdom of France; indeed, he would abandon the ungrateful French to their illnesses forever. Marie-Antoinette, apparently influenced by mesmerist courtiers like the Comte de Ségur, intervened to rescue her people by having Maurepas and other government officials negotiate with Mesmer in March and April 1781. The government offered Mesmer a life pension of 20,000 livres and another 10,000 a year to set up a clinic, if he would but accept the surveillance of three government "pupils." After some complicated negotiations, Mesmer refused with the magniloquent gesture of a public letter to the queen. He shocked Parisians by lecturing Marie-Antionette grandly on "the austerity of my principles." He refused to be judged by his pupils; the offer smacked of bribery, and yet it was not generous enough—he now demanded a country estate, for, after all, what were "four or five hundred thousand francs more or less" to Her Majesty?[2]

It was money, nonetheless, that kept Mesmer in France through his connection with the Society of Universal Harmony (Société de l'Harmonie Universelle). The society was founded by Nicolas Bergasse, a philosopher-lawyer-hypochondriac from a wealthy commercial family of Lyons, and by his best friend, Guillaume Kornmann, a rich banker from Strasbourg. Bergasse and Kornmann attached themselves to Mesmer's tubs, at the usual price of 10 louis a month, in the spring of 1781. They rallied around their master in September 1782, when Deslon set up his own treatment in Paris and was therefore read out of the movement. Deslon returned to the fold for ten weeks at the end of 1783, only to leave once more when Mesmer refused to reveal his ultimate doctrinal secrets. Bergasse then resolved to protect Mesmer from future schismatics and to satisfy his financial demands by organizing his first twelve disciples into a society with an initiation fee of 100 louis a member. After some difficult bargaining, Mesmer agreed to confide

2. The quotations come from d'Onglée, *Rapport au public*, p. 8, and Mesmer, *Précis historique*, pp. 215–217.

his secrets to the society, which, upon payment to him of 2400 louis, would be free (according to Bergasse's version of the agreement) to reveal them for the benefit of humanity. Whether or not Mesmer was a charlatan, he certainly made the most of his doctrine. By June 1785 he had established himself sumptuously in the Hôtel de Coigny, rue Coq-Héron; he traveled about Paris in an elegant coach; and he had collected 343,764 livres, according to the treasurer of the Society of Harmony. The society itself also prospered. By 1789 the mother organization in Paris had 430 members, and had spawned affiliates in Strasbourg, Lyons, Bordeaux, Montpellier, Nantes, Bayonne, Grenoble, Dijon, Marseilles, Castres, Douai, Nîmes, and at least a dozen other towns.

The burgeoning interest of the public corresponded to the society's growth, for mesmerism's power to entertain, if not to cure, was beyond dispute. Renegade followers of Mesmer often offered the public fascinating glimpses of his doctrinal secrets in letters like those Galart de Montjoie published in the *Journal de Paris* in February and March 1784. C. L. Berthollet, the famous chemist, raised a storm by stalking out of Mesmer's treatment, shouting that the cures were produced by the imagination; and the *Courier de l'Europe* disclosed that they were done by sulphur. These revelations only increased the public's excitement. Those who could not afford the price of Mesmer's own explanation of his magical powers could at least learn about his equipment and techniques from counterfeit tubs and pictures that were hawked in the streets. If the cartoons in the collections of the Bibliothèque Nationale represent accurately

A mesmerist charlatan, his pocket bulging with money, puts a helpless beauty into a state of somnambulism. It was widely believed that mesmerizing was a sort of sexual magic, and a secret report by the royal commission on animal magnetism warned the king about its threat to morality.

LE DOIGT MAGIQUE
OU LE MAGNÉTISME ANIMAL

Simius semper Simius

the interests of the 1780's, Parisians cared only about mesmerism, balloon flights, and spectacular feats of heroism or humanitarianism. The salacious character of these cartoons helped imaginations dwell on such interesting topics as, What went on in the crisis room? Why did men usually mesmerize women, and why usually on the hypochondria? Popular songs and doggerels also fed such interests with refrains like:

> *Que le charlatan Mesmer,*
> *Avec un autre frater*
> *Guérisse mainte femelle;*
> *Qu'il en tourne la cervelle,*
> *En les tâtant ne sais où*
> > *C'est fou*
> > *Très fou*
> *Et je n'y crois pas du tout.*

Or:

> *Vieilles, jeunes, laides, belles,*
> *Toutes aiment le docteur,*
> *Et toutes lui sont fidèles.*

The punch line of the most widely reproduced doggerel, in the version that circulated in the *Petites Affiches*, went:

> *Si quelqu'esprit original*
> *Persiste encore dans son délire,*
> *Il sera permis de lui dire:*
> *Crois au magnétisme . . . animal.*

The hangers-on of the Café du Caveau, a gathering place of gossip and news, propagated a promesmerist version of the same song, which ended: "Loin du magnétisme . . . animal." More prosaic hack writers fired imaginations with pamphlets like *La philosophie des vapeurs, ou corre-*

spondance d'une jolie femme and *Le moraliste mesmérien,* which concluded, "In short, the renowned author of the discovery of animal magnetism has done for love what Newton did for the theory of the cosmos."[3]

The movement also thrived on reports of spectacular incidents that made the rounds of the cafés and salons and were ultimately recorded in the *Mémoires secrets.* In December 1784, for example, a young man broke into the royal levee and threw himself at the king's feet, imploring deliverance from the "demon that possesses me; it's that knave Mesmer who has bewitched me." Father Hervier, one of Mesmer's most active supporters, inter-

---

3. On Berthollet's experience with mesmerism, see *Mémoires secrets,* May 26, 1784, pp. 13–14. The cartoons are in the Cabinet des Estampes of the Bibliothèque Nationale, especially the collections Hennin and Vinck (Qb I, Ye 228). They show scenes around the tubs and caricatures of Mesmer, sometimes with a faraway look in his eye and a laudatory verse printed underneath him, sometimes in animal form, pawing a fainting woman. Several cartoons concern the Affaire du Collier, but few between 1780 and 1787 could be considered political. The doggerels come from *Mémoires secrets,* January 17, 1785, pp. 45–46; *Le mesmérisme, ou épitre à M. Mesmer* (a song sheet of 1785, followed by untitled couplets); and a printed *Impromptu fait au Café du Caveau.* They may be translated, respectively, as follows: "That the charlatan Mesmer,/With another confrere/Should cure many a female;/That he should turn their heads,/In touching them I know not where,/It's crazy/Very crazy/And I don't believe in it at all"; "Old ones, young ones, ugly ones, beauties,/All love the doctor,/And all are faithful to him"; and "If some eccentric spirit/Persist still in his folly,/It will be permissible to say to him:/Believe in magnetism . . . animal." The last line of the promesmerist version is translated "Away from magnetism . . . animal." The final quotation is from *Le moraliste mesmérien, ou lettres philosophiques sur l'influence du magnétisme* (London, 1784), p. 8.

Another cartoon (pages 56–57) takes its theme from the refrain of a popular doggerel. It emphasizes the animality of animal magnetism by portraying Mesmer and his followers as dogs. The gesture of the canine Mesmer, reinforced by music, produces chaos. The placards advertise a sale of mesmerist equipment and *Les Docteurs modernes,* the antimesmerist play.

LES EFFETS DU MA

NE TISME........ANIMAL.

rupted a sermon he was delivering in Bordeaux in order to mesmerize a convulsionary parishioner back to her senses. The "miracle" created a sensation, dividing the town into those who thought Hervier a saint and those who considered him a sorcerer, and it caused him to be suspended from preaching and then reinstated, thanks to the support of the local parlement.[4]

Even more spectacular was the discovery or rediscovery of induced hypnosis by the Chastenet de Puységur brothers. They found that a shepherd boy being mesmerized on their estate at Buzancy fell into a strange sleep, stood up, walked, and conversed according to their orders; and they soon learned to produce the most extraordinary effects with this "mesmeric somnambulism." They mesmerized an apparently dead dog back to life. They hypnotized large numbers of peasants tied together around a magnetized tree. And they discovered that a somnambulist could see his own insides while being mesmerized, that he could diagnose his sickness and predict the day of his recovery, that he could even communicate with dead or distant persons. By the autumn of 1784 the Marquis de Puységur was mesmerizing on a huge scale with the enthusiastic support of local officials in Bayonne, and accounts of his feats circulated throughout the nation along with records of cures performed by straight mesmerizing.[5]

4. *Mémoires secrets*, December 3, 1784, p. 56, and April 11, 1784, pp. 258–259; *Remarques sur la conduite du sieur Mesmer, de son commis le P. Hervier, et de ses autres adhérents . . .* (1784); *Lettre d'un Bordelais au Père Hervier . . .* (Amsterdam, 1784); Hervier, *Lettre sur la découverte du magnétisme animal . . .* (Paris, 1784; with an introduction by Court de Gébelin); *Mesmer blessé ou résponse à la lettre du R. P. Hervier sur le magnétisme animal* (1784).

5. *Détail des cures opérées à Buzancy, près Soissons par le magnétisme animal* (Soissons, 1784); J.-M.-P. de Chastenet, Comte de Puységur, *Rapport des cures opérées à Bayonne par le magnétisme animal . . .* (Bayonne, 1784); A. M. J. de Chastenet, Marquis de Puységur, *Mémoires pour servir à l'histoire et à l'établissement du magnétisme animal* (1784). Mesmer claimed to have discovered induced somnambulism but seems not to have practiced it much.

The publicity given to hundreds and hundreds of such carefully documented and often notarized cures must have sapped the faith of many Frenchmen in the purgative potions and bleeding used by conventional doctors. The Comte de Montlosier, a young provincial gentleman, was probably a typical convert to mesmerism. He reacted to the crude religiosity of the Augustinian monks who had directed his early education by devouring the works of the philosophes, adopting somewhat fashionable free-thinking views, and plunging into scientific studies. Newspapers and letters carried the news of the excitement about Mesmer to his estate in Auvergne, where he busied himself with various experiments in the natural sciences. When a student of Deslon's arrived in the neighborhood and promptly cured a woman of a disease that had kept her ill for two years, Montlosier decided to give mesmerizing a try. His instant success inspired him to travel about the countryside, healing peasants and gentlewomen, and to abandon his flirtation with atheism. He had found a deeper, more satisfying kind of science, a science that left room for his religious impulses without excluding his sympathies for philosophy. He had found the "new Paracelsus" called for in the *Encyclopédie*, the romantic, vitalistic science of nature that inspired the dreams of Diderot and of Diderot's d'Alembert. It seemed to Montlosier that mesmerism would "change the face of the world," and this enthusiasm still burned strong in him in 1830. "No event, not even the Revolution, has provided me with such vivid insight as mesmerism."[6]

Mesmerism's hold on the inner life of its partisans can be appreciated from the letters of A.-J.-M. Servan, a well known legal philosopher, a Rousseauist, and a friend and correspondent of Voltaire, d'Alembert, Helvétius, and Buffon. Far from favoring blind leaps into the occult,

6. *Mémoires de M. le comte de Montlosier sur la Révolution Française, le Consulat, l'Empire, la Restauration et les principaux événemens qui l'ont suivie 1755–1830* (Paris, 1830), I, 132–140, quotations from pp. 137, 139.

Servan stressed the need to stick to observable facts, to stand firmly on the ground that had been won from the metaphysicians by Locke and Condillac. Yet his enthusiasm for scientific progress carried him far beyond the limits of experience. The balloon flights had amazed him, he wrote to a nonmesmerist friend; and, "as to electricity, I have an electric machine that amuses me enormously every day; but it astounds me much more. Never have the effects of mesmerism struck me so: if anything should confirm for me the existence of a universal fluid, unique agent in its modifications of so many diverse phenomena, it will be my electric machine. It speaks to me Mesmer's language about nature, and I listen to it with ravishment." Servan's electric machine, like Henry Adams' dynamo, moved him from scientific to religious contemplation. He continued, "For what, after all, are we, sir, in our most exquisite sentiments as in our most vast thoughts; what are we, if not a more or less admirable organ composed of more or fewer stops, but whose bellows never were and never will be in the pineal gland of Descartes nor in the medullary substance of [illegible name], nor in the diaphragm, where certain dreamers have placed it, but in the very principle that moves all the universe? Man, with his liberty, walks only to the cadence of all nature, and all nature moves only to that of a single cause; and what is that cause if not a truly universal fluid, which penetrates all of nature?"[7]

If they drew back from such speculation, serious thinkers nonetheless felt compelled to take mesmerism

7. Servan to M.-A. Julien, August 17, 1781 (probably Servan's copy of the original letter), Bibliothèque municipale, Grenoble, R 1044. Servan's other letters show the same combination of cautious empiricism and mystic deism. See, for example, a letter of April 16, 1788 (Grenoble N 1761), written when Mesmer was visiting him, in which he warned against distorting Mesmer's ideas into an occult, metaphysical system, and a letter to Julien dated only "ce 11 mars" (R 1044), in which he discussed the "premier agent physique, lequel est dans les mains de l'agent des agents et de l'être des êtres; celui qui ne veut remonter qu'à l'agent physique est un spinoziste à tous les diables."

seriously, for the persuasiveness of its advocates and the pervasiveness of its vogue forced men to examine their scientific and religious principles. Condorcet, who typifies so many attitudes of the Enlightenment, rejected mesmerism, but he felt a need to justify his rejection and to put his reasons down in writing. Mesmer had converted some distinguished men, including doctors and physicists, Condorcet noted; moreover, distinguished men had often shown a penchant for "extraordinary facts." How then was one to separate fact from fiction in the systems clamoring for one's allegiance? It was a question that plagued the philosophers of the eighteenth century, and Condorcet had no satisfactory answer to it. "The only witnesses one must believe concerning extraordinary facts are those who are competent judges of them." But who, in the clash of conflicting testimony, could be considered a competent judge-witness? Only the man with a "well-established reputation," Condorcet concluded, conceding, "That is hard for human reason." Not hard but outrageous, was to be the reply of the mesmerists. For if the legitimacy of the systems swarming in France were to be determined by the respectability of the men who testified in their favor, no ideas would survive outside the magic circle of the academies and salons.[8]

Thus mesmerism represented something more than a passing fashion. It might even be viewed as a lay revival of Jansenism (Meister compared Servan's mesmerist writing with Pascal's *Provinciales*). It cut to the core of contemporary attitudes, exposing the need for authority in the vague, speculative area where science and religion met. Seen in the privacy of personal letters and diaries, it appears as an affair of conscience, a challenge to the imperfect arrangement of the thoughtful man's beliefs. Seen in the polemical literature that brought it before the public, it appears as a challenge to authority—not only to Hervier's superiors in the church, but also to the

8. See the selection from Condorcet's manuscripts in Appendix 6.

established scientific bodies and even to the government. By the spring of 1784, when the *Journal de Bruxelles* wondered whether mesmerism "soon will be the sole universal medicine," the government had reason to fear that it was getting out of hand—especially because, as we shall see, the Paris police had submitted a secret report that some mesmerists were mixing radical political ideas in their pseudoscientific discourses.[9] "Never did the tomb of Saint Médard attract more people or produce more extraordinary things than mesmerism. At last it has won the attention of the government," remarked the *Mémoires secrets* on April 24, 1784, in an account of the appointment of a royal commission to investigate mesmerism—or, as Mesmer and his followers believed, to crush it with a blow from the most prestigious and most prejudiced scientists in France.

Prestigious indeed, the commission consisted of four prominent doctors from the faculty of medicine, including Guillotin, and five members of the Academy of Sciences, including Bailly, Lavoisier, and the celebrated Benjamin Franklin. The government also appointed a commission of five members from the faculty's rival, the Royal Society of Medicine, which condemned mesmerism in a report of its own separate investigation. The first commission, however, attracted the most attention. Undeterred by an open letter from Mesmer to Franklin disavowing Deslon's version of animal magnetism, the commissioners spent weeks listening to Deslon lecture on theory and observing his patients fall into convulsions and trances. They underwent continuous mesmerizing themselves, with no effect, and then determined to test the operation of Deslon's fluid outside the excitable atmosphere of his clinic. They found that a false report that she was being mesmerized through a door caused a woman patient to have a "crisis." Another "sensitive" patient was led up to each of five trees, one of which

9. *Journal de Bruxelles*, May 1, 1784, p. 36. Meister's comparison of Servan with Pascal is in Grimm's *Correspondance littéraire*, XIV, 82.

Le Magnétisme dévoilé

The report of the royal commission, brandished by Benjamin
Franklin, confounds the mesmerists, who escape with their loot
in the manner of mountebanks, leaving a wrecked "tub" behind.

Deslon had mesmerized, in Franklin's garden at Passy; he fainted at the foot of the wrong one. Four normal cups of water were held before a Deslon patient at Lavoisier's house; the fourth cup produced convulsions, yet she calmly swallowed the mesmerized contents of a fifth cup, which she believed to be plain water. A series of such experiments, reported in a lucid, rational manner, buttressed the commission's conclusion: Mesmer's fluid did not exist; the convulsions and other effects of mesmerizing could be attributed to the overheated imaginations of the mesmerists.[10]

The report only made the mesmerists boil over in a flood of works defending their cause, the cause of humanity, as they saw it, against a cabal of self-interested academicians. In pamphlet after pamphlet they repeated the same arguments. The commission exposed its bias by refusing to investigate the orthodox doctrine practiced by Mesmer; the imagination alone could not produce the extraordinary effects of mesmerizing; the commissioners had neglected the most important evidence of the fluid's power, the hundreds of cures it had performed; and, in any case, nothing could be more certain than the lethal character of conventional medicine. These pamphlets make dreary reading today, but their very bulk testifies to the passions aroused by the report in 1784.[11]

10. *Rapport des commissaires chargés par le Roi de l'examen du magnétisme animal,* drafted by Bailly (Paris, 1784); *Rapport des commissaires de la Société Royale de Médecine, nommés par le Roi pour faire l'examen du magnétisme animal* (Paris, 1784). A secret report to the King by the Bailly commission also warned that mesmerism could damage morality. Ironically, the one-hundred-third member of the Society of Harmony was Franklin's foppish grandson, William Temple Franklin. On Franklin's role in the mesmerist controversy, see C.-A. Lopez, *Mon Cher Papa: Franklin and The Ladies of Paris* (New Haven, 1966), pp. 168–175.

11. The best argued and most often cited attacks on the commission's report, aside from the works of Bergasse, were: J.-B. Bonnefoy, *Analyse raisonnée des rapports des commissaires chargés par le Roi de l'examen du magnétisme animal* (Lyons, 1784); J.-M.-A. Servan, *Doutes d'un provincial proposés à MM. les médecins commissaires chargés par le Roi de l'examen du magnétisme animal* (Lyons, 1784); J.-F. Fournel, *Remontrances des malades aux médecins de la faculté de Paris* (Amsterdam, 1785).

Passions were further inflamed by an antimesmerist campaign of ridicule, "that weapon with so sure
an effect on us," as the *Journal de Paris* remarked on
November 27, 1784, in reporting the opening of *Les
Docteurs Modernes* at the Comédie Italienne. The play
obviously burlesqued Deslon ("le docteur"), Mesmer
("Cassandre," a shameless swindler: "Peu m'importe
que l'on m'affiche/Partout pour pauvre médecin, / Si je
deviens médecin riche"), and their followers, played by
the chorus, which sang the finale while making a "chain"
around a mesmerist tub. *Les Docteurs Modernes* ran for
21 performances, an enormous success for such a topical
affair. It provided material for endless gossip, essays by
literary pundits like La Harpe, and a bitter counterattack
by Mesmer's supporters. The counterattack was led by
Jean-Jacques d'Eprémesnil, the future leader of the attacks
on the government in the Parlement of Paris. D'Eprémesnil
denounced the play as slander in a pamphlet that he had
thrown into the audience from the third loge during one
of the first performances. He tried to get the Parlement,
the police, the king himself to suppress such an outrage,
but without success; so he published a manifesto de-
claring his own faith in mesmerism and had it thrown
into the audience attending another performance. "Magistrate, but pupil of M. Mesmer, if my personal position
does not permit me to extend to him directly the aid of
the law, at least I owe him, in the name of humanity,
for his person and for his discovery, a public testimonial
of my admiration and of my gratitude, and I hereby give
it." Another mesmerist even attempted to break up a
performance by having his lackey create a disturbance.
The lackey, however, whistled at the wrong play, not
understanding that there was a double bill. Nothing could
prevent the jibes of the play and the antimesmerist
pamphlets and poems from checking the movement's
momentum. Thomas Jefferson—the United States' representative in France whose firm rationalism made him
consider mesmerism "an imputation of so grave a nature

as would bear an action at law in America"—noted tersely in his journal of letters on February 5, 1785, "Animal magnetism dead, ridiculed."[12]

Mesmerism was far more alive than Jefferson realized, for it continued strongly until the Revolution. Although the number of pamphlets declined after 1785, two Parisian theaters considered mesmerism topical enough to produce imitations of *Les Docteurs Modernes* in 1786: *La physicienne* and *Le médecin malgré tout le monde*. On December 11, 1784, the *Journal de Bruxelles* reported on the resiliency of Mesmer's doctrine. "It withstands even the most biting shafts of ridicule. If the capital makes merry with the truly comic scenes of the tub, the provinces have taken them seriously: that's where the really heated practitioners are." Judging from the accounts of cures that poured out of local mesmerist centers, the provinces carried the main impetus of the movement from 1786 to 1789. A correspondent of the Royal Society of Medicine in Castres wrote in 1785, for example, that even the coolest heads in town talked of nothing but mesmerism, and a letter from Besançon printed in the *Mémoires secrets* of March 24, 1786, said, "You won't be able to believe what rapid progress mesmerism has made in this town. Everyone is involved with it." A vast survey published by the antimesmerist Royal Society of Medicine in 1785 showed that few sizable towns in France lacked mesmerist treatments. Leading mesmerists like d'Eprémesnil spread the faith throughout the country, and Mesmer himself

12. *Les Docteurs Modernes, comédie-parade en un acte et en vaudeville suivie du Baquet de Santé, divertissement analogue, mêlé de couplets* . . . (the quotation says, "Little do I care that I am proclaimed/Everywhere as a poor doctor,/If I become a rich doctor" [Paris, 1784], p. 5); J.-J. Duval d'Eprémesnil, *Réflexions préliminaires à l'occasion de la pièce intitulée les Docteurs Modernes* . . . and *Suite des Réflexions préliminaires à l'occasion des Docteurs Modernes* (quotation from pp. 5–6); *The Papers of Thomas Jefferson,* ed. J. P. Boyd (Princeton, 1950–   ), VII, 635. For contemporary accounts of the *Docteurs Modernes* affair, see *Journal de Paris,* November 18, 27, and 28, 1784, pp. 1355, 1405, 1406, 1410, and 1411, and January 18, 1785, p. 76; La Harpe, *Correspondance littéraire,* IV, 266; Grimm's *Correspondance littéraire,* XIV, 76–78; *Mémoires secrets,* November 23, 1784, p. 29.

made a triumphal tour of the societies of harmony in the southern provinces in the spring of 1786. By then the Société Harmonique des Amis Réunis of Strasbourg, one of the most active groups, was wading into the deep waters of spiritualism under the protection of A.-C. Gérard, the head of the local magistracy, who had written to a friend after his initiation into the doctrine in Paris: "I have taken a lot of trouble to be instructed . . . and I have formed the conviction not only of the existence but of the utility of this agent; and since I am impelled by the desire to procure all possible advantages for our city, I have conceived some ideas in this respect that I will communicate to you when they are a little digested." In 1787 the Swedenborgian Exegetical and Philanthropic Society of Stockholm sent a long letter and a Swedenborgian brochure promising a vaster range of spiritual experience to the mesmerists of Strasbourg. Angels had possessed the inner beings of somnambulists in Stockholm, communicating "an adumbration, though feeble, of the first immediate correspondence with the invisible world," the letter explained. Mesmerism and Swedenborgianism complemented one another perfectly, it maintained, and the societies of Strasbourg and Stockholm should cooperate in the business of regenerating mankind by disseminating one another's works.[13]

13. *Extrait de la correspondance de la Société Royale de Médecine, relativement au magnétisme animal; par M. Thouret* (Paris, 1785), p. 11 and *passim*. The letter of Gérard, Strasbourg's Préteur royal, dated June 8, 1784, and other letters, showing that he used his office as late as May 8, 1787, to promote mesmerism in matters like the appointment of a new member of the university's medical faculty, are in Archives de la ville de Strasbourg, mss AA 2660 and 2662 (see esp. letters of July 10, August 11 and 22, October 3 and 19, 1784). The Swedish letter, dated June 19, 1787, was published by the American mesmerist-Swedenborgian, George Bush, in *Mesmer and Swedenborg . . .* (New York, 1847), quotation from p. 265. D'Eprémesnil wrote the notes to *Rapport des cures opérées à Bayonne par le magnétisme animal . . .* (Bayonne, 1784) and visited the Société de l'Harmonie of Bordeaux in December 1784: "Durant huit séances de plusieurs heures chacune, ce magistrat célèbre a exposé le système de M. Mesmer avec une clarté, une force et une noblesse qui transportaient les auditeurs" (*Recueil d'observations et de faits relatif au magnétisme animal . . .* [Philadelphia, 1785], p. 65).

The Lyons brand of mesmerism resembled the Strasbourg variety, as was to be expected, for the leading
mystics of the two cities, men like Jean-Baptiste Willermoz,
Perisse Duluc, Rodolphe Saltzmann, and Bernard de
Turckheim, were united by masonic ties. The *lyonnais*,
however, practiced a unique technique of locating a
patient's disease, without touching him, from the sensations felt by the mesmerizer. Led by the Chevalier de
Barberin, they mesmerized ailing horses in this fashion,
confirming their diagnoses to their own satisfaction, if
not to others', by autopsies, and so provided an answer
to the charge that mesmerizing merely affected the
imagination, a faculty that the "beast-machine" pre-
sumably lacked. The *lyonnais* also prided themselves on
J.-H.-D. Petetin's discovery of induced catalepsy, a state
in which patients sometimes saw their own insides.
Petetin's followers opened the way to the painless hyp-
notic tooth extractions and amputations that provoked
mesmerist controversies well into the nineteenth century.
But the most provocative variety of mesmerism in Lyons
was connected with the spiritualist cults that had taken
root in its traditionally mystic soil. The Lyons mesmerist
society, La Concorde, blossomed with Rosicrucians,
Swedenborgians, alchemists, cabalists, and assorted
theosophists recruited largely from the masonic Ordre
des Chevaliers Bienfaisants de la Cité Sainte. Many of
these mystic masons also staffed the Loge Elue et Chérie,
a spiritualist secret society which prepared to propagate
the true, primitive religion from hieroglyphic messages
received from God by its founder, J.-B. Willermoz. God
was also speaking to Willermoz through the somnambulists of the Concorde, the traditional mysteries of the
Chevaliers Bienfaisants, and other theosophic groups,
including the martinist Ordre des Chevaliers des Elus
Coëns. Willermoz's intimate friend, Louis-Claude de
Saint-Martin, France's most influential martinist, helped
him coordinate these messages, just as he helped Barberin
and Puységur understand the meaning of their discov-

eries. Saint-Martin was well qualified for his role of metaphysical consultant to mesmerists, for he had followed the movement closely and had joined the Parisian Society of Harmony as its twenty-seventh member on February 4, 1784. But he felt that Mesmer's emphasis on the action of the fluid could lead to materialism and expose his followers to the evil influence of spirits called "astral intelligences." Saint-Martin had learned of the spirits from Martines de Pasqually, the founder of martinism, who preached a mixture of cabalism, Talmudic tradition, and mystic Catholicism, from which Saint-Martin drew the main theme of his own works: the material world was subordinate to a more real spiritual realm in which primitive man once had ruled and into which modern man needed to be "reintegrated." Willermoz's secret messages promised to reveal the primitive religion that would bring about the reintegration. Puységur's somnambulism provided direct contact with the spiritual world, and Barberin's technique of mesmerizing cut the ground from under the old-fashioned "fluidists" by dispensing with any material sort of fluid. Thus Saint-Martin wove the later varieties of mesmerism into a mystical and heavily martinist synthesis which, carried on the wave of enthusiasm for somnambulism, typified mesmerist thinking during the last few years of the Ancien Régime.[14]

14. Examples of the extensive contemporary literature concerning later developments of mesmerism, especially in the provinces, are: Pierre Orelut, *Détail des cures opérées à Lyon* . . . (Lyons, 1784); Michel O'Ryan, *Discours sur le magnétisme animal* (Dublin, 1784); J.-H.-D. Petetin, *Mémoire sur la découverte des phénomènes que présentent la catalepsie et le somnambulisme* (1787); *Réflexions impartiales sur le magnétisme animal* . . . (Geneva, 1784); *Système raisonné du magnétisme universel* . . . by the Ostend society (1786); *Règlements des Sociétés de l'Harmonie Universelle, adoptés* . . . *le 12 mai 1785*; *Extrait des registres de la Société de l'Harmonie de France du 30 novembre 1786*. See also J. Audry, "Le mesmérisme à Lyon avant la Révolution," *Mémoires de l'Académie des sciences, belles-lettres et arts de Lyon*, ser. 3 (1924), XVIII, 57–101; Papus (Gérard Encausse), *Louis-Claude de Saint-Martin* (Paris, 1902); and Alice Joly, *Un mystique lyonnais et les secrets de la franc-maçonnerie 1730–1824* (Mâcon, 1938), a biography of Willermoz which takes a sensible, well-documented position on the much debated questions of masonry.

As the Revolution approached, mesmerists tended increasingly to neglect the sick in order to decipher hieroglyphics, manipulate magic numbers, communicate with spirits, and listen to speeches like the following, which reportedly introduced a discourse on Egyptian religion to the Society of Harmony of Bordeaux: "Take a glance, my brothers, at the order's harmonic tableau, which covers this mysterious tub. It is the Isiac table, one of the most remarkable antiquities, where mesmerism is seen at its dawning, in the symbolic writing of our first fathers in animal magnetism, to which only mesmerists have the key." By 1786 even the Parisian Society of Harmony had fallen under the control of spiritualists, notably Savalette de Langes, the founder of the mystical Ordre des Philalèthes, who dabbled in every form of occultism that he and his spies could infiltrate. The mother society nonetheless seemed to be too conservative to the hotheads of Lyons. The *lyonnais* severed their ties with Paris, while the *strasbourgeois* maintained their affiliation only after quarreling publicly about their extravagant practice of somnambulism. The more adventuresome of the Parisians were always welcome in the open house for mystics kept by the Duchesse de Bourbon, who mesmerized constantly with Saint-Martin and Bergasse. Bergasse also haunted the spiritualist gatherings at the home of J.-C. Schweizer and his wife Magdalene, who championed the theory of physiognomy developed by their relative, J.-C. Lavater, the Zurich mesmerist-mystic. Other forms of German mysticism, following the route of Cagliostro, poured into France through the Amis Réunis of Strasbourg, and other spiritualists, Jacques Cazotte, for example, spread their doctrines among the French mesmerists. The Baronne d'Oberkirch, an intimate of mesmerist circles in Paris and Strasbourg, described several séances of these groups and concluded, in a passage evidently written in 1788, "Never, certainly, were Rosicrucians, alchemists, prophets, and everything related to them so numerous and so influential. Conversation turns almost entirely upon these matters; they fill everyone's thoughts; they strike everyone's imagination ... Looking around us, we see only sorcerers, initiates, necromancers, and prophets. Everyone has his own, on whom he counts."[15]

By 1789 this eclectic, spiritualist form of mesmerism, the form that was to be revived in the nineteenth century, had spread throughout Europe. Mesmer's ideas had escaped his control and had run wildly through supernatural regions where he believed they had no business. But by then he had left France in order to search for more fortune in travels to England, Austria, Italy, Switzerland, and Germany, where he died near his birthplace

15. J. B. Barbéguière, *La maçonnerie mesmérienne* ... (Amsterdam, 1784), p. 63 (the quotation is typical of this kind of mesmerism, although the source is unreliable); *Mémoires de la baronne d'Oberkirch sur la cour de Louis XVI et la société française avant 1789* ... ed. Comte de Montbrison (Brussels, 1854), II, 67–77, 158–166, 294–299 (quotation from p. 299). See also Comte Ducos, *La mère du duc d'Enghien, 1750–1822* (Paris, 1900), pp. 199–207, and, for more evidence of popular occultism, the *Journal des gens du monde* (1785), IV, 34, and (1784), I, 133. On the Schweizer-Lavater group, see David Hess, *Joh. Caspar Schweizer: ein Charakterbild aus dem Zeitalter der französischen Revolution*, ed. Jakob Baechtold (Berlin, 1884), and G. Finsler, *Lavaters Beziehungen zu Paris in den Revolutionsjahren 1789–1795* (Zurich, 1898). The societies of Paris and Strasbourg publicized their quarrel in *Extrait des registres de la Société de l'Harmonie de France du 4 janvier 1787* and *Exposé des cures opérées depuis le 25 d'août* (Strasbourg, 1787). Like d'Eprémesnil, Bergasse experimented with many kinds of occultism. His papers in the Château de Villiers, Villiers, Loir-et-Cher, include his copy of Saint-Martin's mystic work, *Des erreurs et de la vérité*, and a letter he wrote on March 21, 1818, which shows that he was then involved in a project to reprint Saint-Martin's works. In a letter to his fiancée of May 7, 1789, he described himself as "presqu'aussi physionomiste que Lavater." The papers also contain Bergasse's draft of his sketch of Jacques Cazotte, published in Michaud's *Biographie Universelle*, which shows a detailed knowledge of the mystical sects at the end of the Ancien Régime. Cazotte, an influential, martinist man of letters, wrote a mesmerist work published as *Témoignage spiritualiste d'outre-tombe sur le magnétisme humain, Fruit d'un long pèlerinage, par J.-S. C* ... , *publié et annoté par l'abbé Loubert* ... (Paris, 1864). This aspect of Cazotte's literary career is not treated in the most thorough study of him, E. P. Shaw, *Jacques Cazotte (1719–1792)* (Cambridge, Mass., 1942).

in 1815. Before he may be permitted to wander out of this narrative and into his obscure, postrevolutionary career, it is important to take account of a schism in the Parisian Society of Harmony that brought out the radical strain in the movement. Bergasse's tendency to dominate the meetings of the society had brought him into conflict with Mesmer several times. By July 1784 their quarrels threatened to split the society into hostile factions, but the defense of the common cause against the commission's report restored harmony until November, when a dispute over a proposal to revise its statutes produced a final break. A committee, led by Bergasse, Kornmann, and d'Eprémesnil, demanded the revision in order to provide for the public propagation of the doctrine, now that the subscription for Mesmer had been filled. Mesmer balked, demanded more money, and finally summoned a general assembly of the society in May 1785. The assembly adopted statutes guaranteeing his supreme direction of the movement and the secrecy of his doctrine. Then, despite various maneuvers, efforts to arrange a compromise, and a harangue by d'Eprémesnil in his best parliamentary style, it expelled the Bergasse faction and took over the Hôtel de Coigny. The outcasts summoned a rival assembly, which adopted statutes drafted by d'Eprémesnil, but by June they conceded that Mesmer had kept the loyalty of most members and that their rump organization had collapsed. They continued to meet informally, however, at Kornmann's house, where, freed from the orthodoxy of the Society of Harmony, they developed the social and political aspects of mesmerist theory.[16]

16. See the sources in note 1 above and also *Extrait des registres de la Société de l'Harmonie de France du 30 November 1786*, which balances them with a pro-Mesmer account of the schism and the subsequent reorganization of the Sociétés de l'Harmonie. The papers of the Parisian society in the Bibliothèque historique de la ville de Paris, ms série 84 and Collection Charavay, mss 811 and 813, indicate that after the purge of the Bergasse group, it was dominated by Savalette de Langes, de Bondy, de Lavigne, Bachelier d'Ages, Gombault, and the Marquis de Gouy d'Arsy.

Mesmerism did not escape a place in the vast conspiracy that the Abbé Barruel's imagination built into pre-revolutionary France, but the Society of Harmony bore no resemblance to a revolutionary cell.[17] In the first place, as a prospective member observed, the 100-louis initiation fee made "a tremendous obstacle" (un furieux obstacle) to joining. Like the innocuous masonic societies of the time, the Society practiced "perfect equality" in its sessions, which included "persons of all ranks, united by the same tie," as Antoine Servan emphasized in his defense of mesmerizing. Mesmer himself proclaimed grandly, "I am not astonished that the pride of persons of high birth should be wounded by the mixture of social conditions found at my house; but I think nothing of it. My humanity encompasses all ranks of society." But the 100-louis fee limited the society's membership almost exclusively to the wealthy bourgeoisie and aristocracy. Even the egalitarianism of its sessions could be factitious, as an antimesmerist pamphlet observed. "The doors close; one is seated according to the order of subscription, and the petty bourgeois who feels for a moment like the equal of a cordon bleu forgets how much his seat of crimson velvet bordered with gold is going to cost him." The exact social composition of the Parisian society cannot be determined, because the standing of all 430 members cannot be traced; but a pamphlet published within a few months of its establishment provides a good idea of its character. The pamphlet said that it then consisted of "48 persons, among whom there are 18 gentle-

17. See Abbé Augustin de Barruel, *Conjuration contre la religion catholique et les souverains* . . . (Paris, 1792), p. 161, and *Mémoires pour servir à l'histoire du jacobinisme* (Hamburg, 1803), V, 93, and remarks on Bergasse in II, 317–323; J. P. L. de Luchet, *Essai sur la secte des illuminés* (Paris, 1789), pp. 21–22, 85. Bergasse said that Barruel based part of his memoirs "sur le témoignage d'un scélérat qui se faisait appeler le Marquis de Beaupoil et que Kornmann fut obligé de chasser de chez lui, après l'avoir nourri par commisération, parce qu'il découvrit qu'il nous trahissait de la manière la plus infâme" (undated letter to his wife, in papers at the Château de Villiers).

men, almost all of eminent birth; 2 knights of Malta; one lawyer of unusual merit; 4 doctors; 2 surgeons; 7 to 8 bankers or merchants, some retired; 2 clergymen; 3 monks." Information available on the provincial societies suggests that they had fewer aristocrats. The 59 members of the Harmony of Bordeaux, for example, included 20 merchants, 10 doctors, and only 2 aristocrats; and the thoroughly bourgeois Harmony of Bergerac later developed into the local Jacobin club. But the Parisian society included some of the greatest aristocrats in France—the Duc de Lauzun, the Duc de Coigny, the Baron de Talleyrand (cousin of the future foreign minister), and the Marquis de Jaucourt, for example—and its members often boasted about the number of courtiers among themselves in order to establish the respectability of their cause, which the Comte de Ségur even defended to the queen. Mesmer's ideal of harmony could easily be construed as a formula for political quietism, as was suggested by a mesmerist pamphlet recommending the "blind respect that is due the government." "Haven't we said that any action, even any thought that tends to upset the order of society is contrary to the harmony of nature . . . ?" Another pamphlet appealed to the public with a pastoral tableau, where a mesmerist "lord of the manor, artlessly and without worry, appears merely to maintain order and to receive homage." Far from harboring a revolutionary cabal, the Society of Harmony provided a sort of fashionable parlor game for the wealthy and the well-bred.[18]

18. The quotations come, respectively, from the diary of the Baron de Corberon, Bibliothèque municipale, Avignon, ms 3059; J.-M.-A. Servan, *Doutes d'un provincial*, p. 7; Mesmer, *Précis historique*, pp. 186–187; *Histoire du magnétisme en France, de son régime et de son influence . . .* (Vienna, 1784), pp. 17, 23; *Nouvelle découverte sur le magnétisme animal . . .* pp. 44–45; *Lettre de M. Axxx à M. Bxxx sur le livre intitulé: Recherches et doutes sur le magnétisme animal de M. Thouret* (1784), p. 21. The full membership list of the Parisian society is in *Journal du magnétisme* (Paris, 1852). The members that can be identified from it were wealthy bourgeois and aristocrats. The members of the Bordeaux society are

The society's organization and ceremonies confirm this judgment. Even Mesmer's treatment suggested the high status of his clientele. One of his four tubs was reserved, without charge, for the poor and was rarely used, but places at the other three had to be booked well in advance like seats in the opera, and they reportedly brought in 300 louis a month. Flowers set apart the tub for "ladies of breeding," and Mesmer's German doorman was said to announce arrivals with three kinds of whistles, which varied according to the patient's social standing. The society met in the Hôtel de Coigny, where Mesmer lived and conducted his treatments. Its officers varied, but they usually were: perpetual president, Mesmer, whose faulty French limited his participation in meetings; vice presidents, Adrien Duport, the member of Parlement and future Feuillant leader, and the Marquis de Chastellux, the prominent soldier and man of letters; orator, Bergasse, sometimes aided by others; treasurer, Kornmann; one or two masters of ceremonies; an archivist, and from one to four secretaries. Each member received an elaborate diploma from Mesmer, which bound him to secrecy and certified his place in the hierarchy of disciples: Bergasse was first, Kornmann second, Duport thirty-fourth, Lafayette ninety-first, and d'Eprémesnil one-hundred-thirty-sixth. Bergasse, who dominated the society's meetings, claimed that he in-

named in *Recueil d'observations,* and the society of Bergerac is studied in Henri Labroue, *La société populaire de Bergerac avant la Révolution . . .* (Paris, 1915). The more frivolous character of the Parisian society was well described in *L'Antimagnétisme . . .* (London, 1784), p. 3: "Ce goût pour les choses voilées, à sens mystique, allégorique, est devenu général dans Paris et occupe aujourd'hui presque tous les gens aisés . . . Mais le magnétisme animal, considéré en grand, est dans ce moment le joujou le plus à la mode et qui fait remuer le plus de têtes." See also Grimm's *Correspondance littéraire,* XIII, 510–515; the Comte de Ségur, *Mémoires ou souvenirs et anecdotes* (Paris, 1829), II, 60–61; *Système raisonné du magnétisme universel . . .* (1786), p. 97, which printed the society's rules of 1786 providing for "la liberté et l'égalité dans les avis des membres."

tended them to be purely philosophical in character; but, "I was asked to provide by-laws for this society, which at first was given, in spite of my wishes, the ridiculous denomination of *lodge*."[19]

The sessions, initiation rites, and instruction courses involved a combination of occult science and masonic-like ritual, as can be judged from some excerpts from the diary of the Baron de Corberon, who wrote the only direct account of the society's activities (see Appendix 3). Corberon noted a strong masonic influence on the formal meetings in the assembly room of the Hôtel de Coigny, but his descriptions of the instruction courses rather resemble reports of the scientific lectures in the Parisian museums and lyceums. Bergasse adopted a professorial manner with the neophytes. He lectured with a pointer, drew elaborate diagrams, arranged wax balls to represent the movement of atoms through space, and even wrote a sort of parody of a scientific textbook, complete with illustrations of colliding molecules, currents of magnetism, and such other attracting, repelling, expanding, whirling fluids as light, heat, gravity, and electricity. In the induction ceremony, the new members recited a religious oath and placed themselves in mesmeric "rapport" with the director of the ceremony, who embraced them, saying, "Go forth, touch, cure" (Allez, touchez, guérissez). After the initiations, Corberon related, the neophytes were divided into two study groups, which met three days a week during the next month, in order to prepare for full membership. The eleven sessions that

19. Bergasse's remark is in his *Observations*, p. 17. For details on the Société de l'Harmonie, see *Histoire du magnétisme en France . . .* (Vienna, 1784) and *Testament politique de M. Mesmer . . .* (Leipzig, 1785). Some of the society's papers, an incomplete collection of the diplomas, different sorts of contracts between Mesmer and his students, correspondence, mostly from 1786, attendance records, and other documents are in the Bibliothèque historique de la ville de Paris, ms série 84 and Collection Charavay, mss 811 and 813.

Corberon attended consisted mainly of lectures by Bergasse that corresponded generally to the argument he published in his *Considérations sur le magnétisme animal*. Bergasse explained the three basic principles, God, matter, and movement; the mesmeric fluid's action among planets, within all bodies, and particularly within man; the techniques of mesmerizing; illness and its cures; the nature of instinct; and the occult knowledge obtainable through the fluid's action on man's inner sense. Corberon observed that Bergasse dominated the sessions to the extent that "there are plenty of sympathetic spirits in Paris who would like to 'Bergassize' as much as to 'mesmerize.'" The surviving papers of the society show no more signs of political activities than does Corberon's journal. The 103 letters remaining from its vast correspondence consist mainly of routine applications for membership, usually full of the humanitarian expressions common at the time. Typical was a letter from a M. Oliviez, who wrote that he possessed "good fluid" and wanted to use it to "relieve suffering humanity."[20]

The Society of Harmony had originated as a project to secure the survival of Mesmer's doctrine and fortune when they were threatened by academic bodies and the government. By the time of its schism, it had become flooded with aristocrats, eminent bourgeois, and even an academician, the Marquis de Chastellux, who wrote an essay, published in Bergasse's *Considérations sur le magnétisme animal*, on the mesmeric, antigravitational, "special secretions of the globe." Such collaboration probably opened the doors to some fashionable salons, and Bergasse may have welcomed it, but his expulsion slammed these doors shut and developed in him a revulsion against the fashionable, well-bred variety of mes-

20. The induction ceremony is described in the Ostend society, *Système raisonné du magnétisme universel*, p. 110. The letters, from 1786, are in the Bibliothèque historique de la ville de Paris, ms série 84.

merism. He and his expelled friends denounced "that discordant species" (cette espèce criard) in several pamphlets accusing Mesmer of exploiting his discovery for financial gain and of failing in his duty to publicize his secrets for the benefit of humanity. They themselves fulfilled this duty by giving a public lecture course on mesmerism from the summer of 1785 until at least the spring of 1787. The lectures, mostly by Bergasse and d'Eprémesnil, departed considerably from Mesmer's ideas, as Bergasse indicated. "I have overturned the foundations of his system and I have raised on the ruins of that system an edifice that is, I believe, far more vast and more solidly constructed." Liberated from the confining organization and dogma of the Society of Harmony, Bergasse developed the social and political aspects of his theory—his own ideas about "universal morality, about the principles of legislation, about education, habits, the arts, etc.," as he put it, in summarizing his differences with Mesmer. Bergasse and his friends developed these ideas more boldly in the privacy of informal gatherings at Kornmann's house, where Bergasse, then a bachelor, lived until the Revolution. The Kornmann group reviled Mesmer for betraying the movement's original fight against the "despotism of the academies," and they extended this fight into the larger battle against political despotism.[21]

There is no description of the group just after the schism, but it probably included Kornmann, Bergasse, d'Eprémesnil, Lafayette, and Adrien Duport. By the time of its greatest activity, 1787–1789, it had neglected mes-

21. Nicolas Bergasse, *Considérations sur le magnétisme animal* . . . (The Hague, 1784), p. 148; Bergasse, *Observations,* pp. 53–54, 73; Bergasse, *Supplément aux Observations,* pp. 20, 27. Mesmer himself identified the tendency of the schismatics' doctrine in his *Lettre de l'auteur de la découverte du magnétisme animal,* p. 2: "Auriez-vous l'orgueilleuse prétention de créer . . . une nouvelle logique, une nouvelle morale, une nouvelle jurisprudence?"

merism in order to devote itself fully to the political crisis, and it had acquired nonmesmerist members like the future Girondist leaders Etienne Clavière and Antoine-Joseph Gorsas. Jacques-Pierre Brissot joined the group in the summer of 1785. Impressed by the general fascination with mesmerism and the persuasive tone of mesmerist writings, he sought out Bergasse, who converted him to the cause with demonstrations of "several very extraordinary facts" and began seeing him almost daily in "the very closest friendship." Brissot wrote his mesmerist manifesto, *Un mot à l'oreille des académiciens de Paris,* as an intimate of the Kornmann group, for he dashed it off after an inspired "soulful session" (épanchement) with Bergasse, and he filled it with praises of Bergasse and d'Eprémesnil without even mentioning Mesmer. "Bergasse did not hide from me the fact that in raising an altar to mesmerism, he intended only to raise one to liberty. 'The time has now come,' he used to say to me, 'for the revolution that France needs. But to attempt to produce one openly is to doom it to failure; to succeed it is necessary to wrap oneself in mystery, it is necessary to unite men under the pretext of experiments in physics, but, in reality, for the overthrow of despotism.' It was with this in mind that he formed in Kornmann's house, where he was living, a society of men who spoke openly about their desire for political change. This group included Lafayette, d'Eprémesnil, Sabathier, etc. There was another smaller group of writers, who used their pens to prepare that revolution. It was at the dinners that the most important questions were discussed. I used to preach republicanism there; but, with the exception of Clavière, no one appreciated it. D'Eprémesnil only wanted to 'de-Bourbonize' France (this was his expression) in order to bring her under the rule of the Parlement. Bergasse wanted a king and two chambers, but above all he wanted to draft the plan himself and to have it rigorously executed: his mania was to believe himself a Lycurgus.

"There is no denying that the efforts of Bergasse and those who assembled in his [Kornmann's] house have contributed singularly to speeding up the revolution. One cannot calculate the number of tracts that it produced. It was from this source that almost all the works published against the ministry in 1787 and 1788 were released, and one should give Kornmann his due: he consecrated part of his fortune to these publications. Several of them came from Gorsas, who was then trying out the satirical pen with which he has so often slashed apart monarchism, autocracy, feuillantism and anarchy. Carra also distinguished himself in those combats, in which I participated to a certain extent."[22]

The key role played by the Kornmann group during the Prerevolution lies outside the limits of this study, but it should be noted as an example of the final stage in the evolution of a radical strain within the fashionable, apolitical movement of mesmerism in general, and its existence raises this question: what was it in mesmerism that appealed to the radical mentality before the Revolution?

22. *Mémoires de J.-P. Brissot (1754–1793), publiés avec étude critique et notes,* ed. Claude Perroud (Paris, 1911), II, 53–56. Like everything else in Brissot's memoirs, these passages are colored by his desire, shortly before his execution, to prove his early devotion to the revolutionary cause. Although Brissot did not name Duport as a member of the group and there is no record of Duport's stand during the schism in the Société de l'Harmonie, Duport, a vice-president of the society at that time, almost certainly aligned himself with the Kornmann group. The records of 1786 in the Bibliothèque historique de la ville de Paris exclude him from the list of officers and members of the "Société de l'Harmonie de France" that was recreated by Mesmer after the schism. Kornmann evidently confided his papers to Duport, because the inventory of Duport's own papers, sequestered during the Revolution, mentioned various mesmerist documents (probably records of the society before the schism, which are missing from the Bibliothèque historique collection) including some receipts "fournies au nommé Korneman [*sic*], mais pour le compte dudit Mesmer, ainsi qu'il paraît par des notes qui

établissent qu'il faisait les affaires dudit Mesmer et cela en l'année 1784" (Archives Nationales, T 1620). A letter from Duport to Bergasse, dated "ce 5 avril," in Bergasse's manuscripts at Villiers, shows that he had a high regard for Bergasse and the "fruit qu'on doit espérer de vos talents et de vos lumières." Duport also associated with members of the Kornmann group in the Société des Trente and the Société Française des Amis des Noirs.

3. THE RADICAL STRAIN IN MESMERISM

When Jacques-Pierre Brissot became a convert to mesmerism in 1785, he had witnessed the Genevan republican revolution of 1782; he had assimilated Rousseau's works—from the *Social Contract* to the songs; he had published his own denunciations of the evils of French society; and he had spent two desperate months in the Bastille. Mesmerism did not offer him new radical ideas. He had already absorbed, applied, and suffered for the Rousseauist views that Bergasse revealed to him in mesmerist theory. Bergasse's vulgarization of Rousseau probably appealed to him as a means of communicating with the vast majority of readers who had never opened the *Social Contract,* and mesmerism in general probably fascinated him for the same reason that it fascinated so many of his contemporaries: it seemed to offer a new scientific explanation of the invisible forces of nature. But the radical strain of mesmerism that Brissot represents developed as a response to another element of the mesmerist movement.

Mesmerist pamphlets constantly portrayed Mesmer as a dedicated man who arrived in Paris with a discovery that would put an end to human suffering and who naively turned to the leading academic and scientific bodies of the country for support. One by one, the Academy of Sciences, the Royal Society of Medicine, the faculty of medicine, and finally a royal commission epitomizing the academic establishment snubbed, humiliated, and persecuted him. Mesmer's offers to have his cures verified and to compete in public treatments with conventional doctors exposed the wickedness of his persecutors. His system threatened a professional corps, which united with other vested interests to annihilate the threat, regardless of the cost in human suffering. Mesmer therefore turned his back on academic officialdom and addressed the nonprofessionals: "It is to the public that I appeal." This popular appeal, sounded in hundreds of pamphlets, alarmed the government, and not without reason, for some mesmerist works developed political overtones: they showed that privileged bodies, supported by the government, were attempting to suppress a movement to improve the lot of the common people. For example, in 1784 Antoine Servan, the radical avocat-général of the Parlement of Grenoble and brother of the future Girondist minister, castigated doctors in terms reminiscent of his outspoken *Apologie de la Bastille:* "[You] maintain ceaselessly the most complete despotism of which man is capable . . . you become absolute sovereigns over the sick common people." In a passionate defense of mesmerism, Brissot lashed out at academicians: "You have been told a hundred times: in crying out against despotism, you have become its firmest supporters, you maintain a revolting despotism yourselves." Overlooking their leader's negotiations with Maurepas, some mesmerists hinted at an evil alliance between the government and the academies to protect the established order. Bergasse represented a doctor of the faculty of medicine demanding state action to prevent medical reform, because, as he said, "It is important to maintain [among the common people], as a constant civilizing influence, all the prejudices that can make medicine respectable . . . The corps of doctors is a political body, whose destiny is linked with that of the state . . . Thus, within the social order, we absolutely must have diseases, drugs and laws, and the distributors of drugs and diseases influence the habits of a nation perhaps as much as do the guardians of its laws." Another mesmerist argued that the defense of the faculty of medicine and the Royal Society of Medicine had become "the policy of the state, for whom it is important to conserve those two bodies." In support of this view, mesmerists noted that the government printed and distributed 12,000 copies of the commission's report, that it circulated reprints of academic resolutions against mesmerism, that it printed a long attack on mesmerism by Thouret, Mesmer's leading enemy in the Royal Society of Medicine, and that it suppressed works in favor of mesmerism. After the commission's report appeared, Mesmer's followers expected an edict outlawing animal magnetism, and Mesmer himself prepared to flee to England as if he were a Linguet or a Raynal escaping from a *lettre de cachet*.[1]

At this point, the most critical in the history of the movement, d'Eprémesnil suggested that Bergasse write a petition in Mesmer's name to the Parlement of Paris. Bergasse complied by denouncing the commission's report for the violation of the most basic rules of justice and morality and "the first principles of natural law." The Parlement should stand up against this royally commissioned lawlessness by placing mesmerism under its special protection, Bergasse wrote. He requested the Parlement to sponsor an honest investigation of mesmerism and called for "the destruction of that fatal science, the oldest superstition of the universe, of that tyrannical medicine which, first seizing man in the cradle, weighs on him like a religious prejudice." The Parlement accepted the petition and appointed its own investigating

1. F. A. Mesmer, *Précis des faits relatifs au magnétisme animal...* (London, 1781), p. 40; J.-M.-A. Servan, *Doutes d'un provincial, proposés à Messieurs les médecins-commissaires...* (Lyons, 1784), pp. 101–102; J.-P. Brissot (anonymously), *Un mot à l'oreille des académiciens de Paris*, pp. 8–9; Nicolas Bergasse, *Lettre d'un médecin de la faculté de Paris à un médecin du collège de Londres...* (The Hague, 1781), p. 65; *Les vieilles lanternes, conte nouveau...* (1785), p. 82. The various academic resolutions condemning mesmerism that were printed and sometimes distributed by the government are in the Bibliothèque Nationale collection, 4° Tb 62, pamphlets 54–58 and 116. For the reaction of the mesmerists to this persecution, see Bergasse, *Lettre de M. Mesmer à Messieurs les auteurs du Journal de Paris et à M. Franklin* (1784); *Lettres sur le magnétisme animal où l'on discute l'ouvrage de M. Thouret...* (Brussels, 1784); Bergasse, *Considérations sur le magnétisme animal...* (The Hague, 1784), pp. 24–25; Bergasse, *Observations de M. Bergasse sur un écrit du docteur Mesmer...* (London, 1785), pp. 24–29. On September 10, 1785, the Chambre syndicale de la librairie et imprimerie de Paris recorded the refusal to permit the publication of a mesmerist book by Deslon, noting in the margin, "Le roi ne veut point que l'on permette d'écrire sur cet objet" (Bibliothèque Nationale, fonds français, 21866). The prohibition was not effective.

commission on September 6, 1784. The investigation never took place, because the commission hesitated to take on its task and was replaced by yet another commission, which apparently never met. But the petition had served its purpose: Bergasse wrote a year later that it "recalled the authorities to their usual circumspection and caution; and henceforth mesmerism and its founder had no more public persecution to fear."[2]

The seriousness of the government's threat to mesmerism and the importance of the Parlement's defense of it can be judged from an excerpt from the manuscript memoirs of Jean-Pierre Lenoir, who was lieutenant-general of police in Paris at the time. "In 1780 the vogue of mesmerism began in Paris. The police were concerned with this ancient practice . . . because of its bearing on morality . . . The government opposed it only with indifference while M. de Maurepas was alive; but some time after his death [1781], the police were warned by anonymous letters that seditious speeches against religion and the government were being made in the meetings of the mesmerists. Then, upon the police's denunciation,

2. Bergasse printed the requête in *Lettre de M. Mesmer à M. le Comte de Cxxx* (1784). The second quotation comes from Bergasse's *Observations*, p. 29. On the Parlement's protection of Mesmer, see also *Mémoires secrets pour servir à l'histoire de la république des lettres en France,* September 12 and 14 and October 6, 1784, pp. 227–230, 231–232, 275; Hardy's journal, Bibliothèque Nationale, fonds français, 6684, entries for September 5 and 7, 1784; and J.-F. La Harpe, *Correspondance littéraire* . . . (Paris, 1801–1807), IV, 272. Several letters by mesmerists in the Joly de Fleury collection of the Bibliothèque Nationale demonstrate their conviction that only the Parlement could protect them from "une persécution méthodique de la part des savants et des sages," as Mesmer and fourteen of his disciples stressed in a letter to the procureur-général dated December 3, 1784 (fonds français, 1690). The letter surveyed the entire mesmerist movement as if it were a struggle against official persecution. In another letter to the procureur-général, dated September 4, 1784 *(ibid.),* Mesmer reported that, "environné de dangers sans cesse renaissants," and as a victim of the "persécution secrète de la part d'un homme puissant," he had appealed to the Imperial ambassador for protection; perhaps he considered fleeing back to Vienna.

one of the king's ministers proposed expelling Mesmer, a foreigner, from the kingdom . . . Other ministers were of the opinion, which got a better reception, that it was in the Parlement that all illicit, immoral and irreligious sects and assemblies should be prosecuted. I was directed to summon the attorney-general. That magistrate answered me that if he lodged a complaint against the mesmerist meetings in the Grande Chambre, it would be referred to the chambres assemblées, where there would be partisans and protectors of mesmerism. Therefore no prosecution was made." Having saved mesmerism at its weakest moment, the Parlement hesitated to propagate it actively, which Bergasse himself neither wanted nor expected.[3]

The Parlement's stand put it in excellent relations with the mesmerists. Although there is no record of how many councillors sympathized with mesmerism, La Harpe observed that half the Parlement supported it, which seems a fairly reliable estimate, since La Harpe attended many mesmerist sessions himself. Of course the Parlement was no revolutionary body, and its support did not brand mesmerism as a radical cause; but it supplied the mesmerists with the only available counterforce to the government, and by 1785 the government struck many mesmerists as the incarnation of evil, for it had persecuted what they believed to be the most

3. Lenoir papers, Bibliothèque municipale, Orléans, ms 1421; Bergasse, *Observations,* pp. 100–101. Like most of the material Lenoir intended to publish as his memoirs, this is in a very crude draft. In another note on the mesmerists (ms 1423), he wrote that, "soutenus par des personnes puissantes, par des courtisans et par des magistrats du Parlement, je n'aurais pas osé les troubler." He became involved with the mesmerists in episodes resembling the Jansenist controversies. For example, he wrote that the vicar of St. Eustache refused to bury Deslon, the schismatic mesmerist, and "M. d'Eprémesnil, conseiller au Parlement et zélé partisan du magnétisme, menaçait de dénoncer le refus du vicaire. Cet incident, que j'évitais au moyen d'une lettre de cachet signifiée au curé de la même paroisse, fit perdre de vue les poursuites ordonnées par M. le Garde des Sceaux, que le procureur-général ne s'était pas pressé de faire" (ms 1421).

humanitarian movement of their age. The Kornmann group expressed its hatred of the government and its indebtedness to the Parlement three years later, when it rallied popular support for the Parlement's opposition to the programs of the Calonne and Brienne ministries and the Parlement's call for the convocation of the Estates General. The important alliance of 1787–1788 between extremist councillors like Duport and d'Eprémesnil and radical pamphleteers like Brissot and Carra first developed around mesmerist tubs.[4]

Lafayette participated actively in this alliance, but he left little indication of his own mesmerist ideology, as he was no writer or speaker but the sort of man who made his appearances in history while mounted on chargers or standing on balconies in front of revolutionary crowds. The written evidence that does exist suggests that his experience of the American Revolution and his friendship with Thomas Jefferson had a strong influence on his political ideas, and further that he saw some connection between his dedication to the American republic and to mesmerism. Even Louis XVI associated these two interests when he asked Lafayette, shortly before the young hero's departure for the United States in June 1784, "What will Washington think when he learns that you have become Mesmer's chief journeyman apothecary?" In fact Washington already knew, for Lafayette had written to him on May 14, 1784: "A German doctor n̲ ̲ ̲d Mesmer, having made the greatest discovery about aniṃ̲.̲ ' magnetism, has trained some pupils, among whom youɪ ʰ°mble servant is considered one of the most enthusiastic.- ᵀ know as much about it as any sorcerer ever did . . . Before

4. La Harpe, *Correspondance littéraire*, IV, 272–275. Bergasse's violent attacks on the government during the Kornmann affair of 1787–1789 provoked the accusation that he was only seeking revenge for the government's persecution of mesmerism (Beaumarchais, *Troisième mémoire, ou dernier exposé des faits* . . . [1789], p. 59).

leaving I will obtain permission to let you into Mesmer's secret, which, you can count on it, is a great, philosophical discovery." Lafayette sailed with Mesmer's special cure for seasickness (he was to hug the mast, which would prevent queasiness by acting as a mesmeric "pole"; this, unfortunately, proved impossible because of a tar coating at the base of the mast) and with a special commission to proselytize for the Society of Harmony, which planned to establish extensive branches in America. Lafayette fulfilled his commission so energetically that Jefferson, then the American representative to Versailles, tried to prevent a wave of mesmerism at home by sending antimesmerist pamphlets and copies of the commission's report to influential friends. Jefferson's efforts reassured Charles Thomson, who wrote that Lafayette had campaigned actively: "He had got a special meeting called of the philosophical society at Philadelphia and entertained them for the better part of an evening. He informed them that he was initiated and let into the secret but was not at liberty to reveal it." Lafayette even included a visit to a colony of Shakers in his campaign, because he took their shaking to be a form of native mesmerism. There is no evidence that he connected mesmerism with radical political ideas, but in 1787 he was associated with Bergasse and Brissot in the Gallo-American Society, a Parisian group that combined its enthusiasm for the United States with attacks on the most prominent French minister, Charles-Alexandre de Calonne; and in 1788 he joined the Gallo-Americans in another club that became a center of radicalism, the Société Française des Amis des Noirs (French Society of the Friends of the Blacks). Of course these associations do not prove that Lafayette was a convinced revolutionary before 1789. Perhaps he only flirted with the radicalism of his bourgeois friends in the spirit of philosophical slumming described by his close friend, the Comte de Ségur. "One finds pleasure in descending, so long as one believes it possible to climb

up again as soon as one pleases; and so, without fore-
sight, we enjoyed simultaneously the advantages of the
patrician order and the charms of a plebeian philosophy."
In the last analysis, Lafayette remained a great aristocrat.
His social position probably prevented him from respond-
ing to the element of mesmerism that most appealed to
future revolutionaries like Jacques-Pierre Brissot and
Jean-Louis Carra.[5]

What attracted these radicals to the movement was
Mesmer's stand against the academic bodies that often
dispensed success or failure for obscure individuals like
themselves, who were scrambling for recognition as men
of letters and science. Mesmer's fight was their fight.

5. Grimm's *Correspondance littéraire*, XIV, 25; Lafayette to Washing-
ton, May 14, 1784, in *Mémoires, correspondances et manuscrits du général
Lafayette publiés par sa famille* (Paris and London, 1837), II, 93; on Lafay-
ette's seasickness, see his letter to his wife, June 28, 1784, in André
Maurois, *Adrienne ou la vie de Madame de Lafayette* (Paris, 1960), p. 150;
Charles Thomson to Jefferson, March 6, 1785, in *The Papers of Thomas
Jefferson*, ed. J. P. Boyd (Princeton, 1950–   ), VIII, 17; Ségur's remark
is in *Mémoires ou souvenirs et anecdotes par M. le comte de Ségur* (Paris,
1829), I, 31. The Reverend James Madison wrote to Jefferson from
Williamsburg on April 10, 1785: "The Marq. Le Fayette [*sic*] in his
journey thro' this town had raised amongst us the highest anxiety to
know the real discoveries made in animal magnetism. But the pamphlet
you favoured us with has effectually quieted our concern upon that
score" (*Papers of Jefferson*, VIII, 73). For other documents of Jefferson's
private campaign against mesmerism, see *ibid.*, VII, 17, 504, 508, 514,
518, 570, 602, 635, 642, VIII, 246, IX, 379. Lafayette's mesmerism is
mentioned in Louis Gottschalk, *Lafayette between the American and
French Revolutions, 1783–1789* (Chicago, 1950), pp. 97–98, and M. de la
Bedoyere, *Lafayette, a Revolutionary Gentleman* (London, 1933), pp.
89–90. A mesmerist plan to establish connections in America was announced in *Nouvelle découverte sur le magnétisme animal . . .* , and the
pro-American attitude of mesmerists was caricatured in *La vision
contenant l'explication de l'écrit intitulé: Traces du magnétisme et la théorie
des vrais sages* (Paris, 1784), p. iv: "Les américains, dont l'organisation
est plus sensible et plus irritable que celle des habitants de l'ancien
monde, accourent de l'autre pôle pour rendre hommage à son [Mesmer's]
art merveilleux." On Lafayette's connections with the Gallo-American
Society and the Amis des Noirs, see *J. P. Brissot, correspondance et
papiers*, ed. Claude Perroud (Paris, 1912), pp. 165–166, 169.

He had won it by attacking the arbiters, the very rules of the game, and his example inspired them to make more audacious attacks, to challenge the order of society as well as the establishment that limited access to its most prestigious positions. This anti-establishment kind of radicalism can best be seen in the mesmerist ideas of Brissot, Carra, and Bergasse.

Throughout Brissot's early works and even his memoirs runs his ambition to make himself, the thirteenth child of a provincial tavern keeper, a philosopher, the equal of any man in the salons and academies of Paris. It was his struggle to satisfy this ambition that aroused his interest in politics, for he came to see the world of philosophers in political terms. "The domain of the sciences must be free from despots, aristocrats and electors. It presents a picture of a perfect republic. In it, merit is the sole claim to honors. To admit a despot or aristocrats or electors . . . is to violate the nature of things, the liberty of the human spirit; it is to make a criminal attempt upon public opinion, which alone has the right to crown genius; it is to introduce a revolting despotism." Brissot's frustrated attempts to win a place for himself as a philosopher, a lawyer, a scientist, and a journalist taught him that ill-born provincial lads cut a sorry figure in Parisian salons, academies, and professions, that the republic of letters had degenerated into a "despotism," where "independent men" like himself, youths lacking wealth and social standing, were repressed and ridiculed. These outcast philosophers carried new truths in their breasts, truths that threatened to disrupt the social order; and therefore Richelieu and his despotic successors had founded academies and stuffed them with men of great wealth, breeding, and ignorance. Liberal governments had no academies. (Brissot conveniently overlooked the existence of the Royal Society and the American Philosophical Society.) A government like that of France used academies to control public opinion, to stifle the new truths of science and philosophy, in short, as a "new prop for its despotism."[6]

Brissot learned this lesson at the feet of a man who epitomized the important but generally unappreciated connection between political radicalism and the frustrated ambitions of the many would-be Newtons and Voltaires of prerevolutionary Paris. This man was Jean-Paul Marat. Brissot was introduced to Marat in 1779 by the Baron de Marivetz, author of *Physique du Monde,* a cosmological fantasy very much like mesmerism, which Marivetz later propagated as a member of the Society of Harmony. By 1782, Brissot had become a devoted friend of Marat's. He championed Marat's scientific theories in articles and conversations; he tried to arrange for the translation and distribution of Marat's books; he apparently even proselytized for Marat by repeating his experiments; and Marat responded with expressions of the warmest friendship: "You know, my very dear friend, what a place you occupy in my heart." The two had much in common. Each left his modest home and ultimately settled in Paris with the ambition of becoming an established philosophe; and each manifested this ambition by adopting aristocratic airs (wearing a sword and attaching an aristocratic suffix to his name) and by struggling in the main channel for self-advancement, the competition for prizes and memberships offered by the academies. Marat, eleven and one-half years Brissot's senior, had struggled longer and could offer his young friend advice: "Frank and just spirits like yours know nothing of the tortuous ways of a despot's satellites, or rather they dis-

6. J.-P. Brissot, *De la vérité, ou méditations sur les moyens de parvenir à la vérité dans toutes les connoissances humaines* (Neuchâtel, 1782), pp. 165–166, 187. *Un indépendant à l'ordre des avocats* (Berlin, 1781), an attack on the corps of lawyers like his mesmerist attack on doctors in 1785, is another expression of Brissot's frustrated ambition at this time, which he described vividly in his memoirs (*J.-P. Brissot, Mémoires (1754–1795),* ed. Claude Perroud [Paris, 1910], e.g. I, 121).

dain them." Marat spoke with the authority of one who had fought for years to win his rightful seat in the Academy of Sciences. That place belonged to him, he felt, because he had wrestled with hundreds of experiments and filled thousands of pages with irrefutable arguments in order to unseat the great Newton and reveal to the world the true nature of light, heat, fire, and electricity—which were produced by invisible fluids rather like Mesmer's.[7]

In fact, Marat's attempt to break into the scientific elite of Paris coincided with Mesmer's. Marat submitted his *Découvertes de M. Marat sur le feu, l'électricité et la lumière* for the academy's approval in 1779, when Mesmer, smarting from his recent humiliation by the academy, was publishing his first *Mémoire* on his own discovery. At first the academy treated Marat more favorably than it had just treated Mesmer, but it turned against him as his subsequent works advanced more extravagant theories and his claims to have outdone Newton became more acrimonious. By the time of the academy's condemnation of Mesmer in 1784, Marat had convinced himself that it was persecuting him, too. Indeed he believed that the

7. Marat to Brissot, undated (1783) in Brissot's *Correspondance*, pp. 78–80; see also Brissot to Marat, June 6, 1782, *ibid.*, pp. 33–35. On the meeting of Brissot and Marat, see Marat's article in *L'Ami du Peuple*, June 4, 1792, reprinted in *Annales révolutionnaires* (1912), p. 685. For Brissot's not very convincing explanation of the suffix "de Warville" that he adopted, see *Réponse de Jacques-Pierre Brissot à tous les libellistes qui ont attaqué et attaquent sa vie passée* (Paris, 1791), p. 5. The best biography of Brissot is still Eloise Ellery, *Brissot de Warville* (Boston, 1915). Marat's career before the Revolution is treated most thoroughly in Cabanès, *Marat inconnu, l'homme privé, le médecin, le savant . . . 2* ed. (Paris, 1911). Louis Gottschalk, in *Jean Paul Marat: A Study in Radicalism* (New York, 1927), interprets Marat's quarrel with the Academy of Sciences as the crucial element in his revolutionary career. This interpretation coincides with Marat's own view, published in his *Le Publiciste de la république française, ou observations aux français* (March 19, 1793): "Vers l'époque de la révolution, excédé des persécutions que j'éprouvais depuis si longtemps de la part de l'Académie des Sciences, j'embrassai avec ardeur l'occasion qui se présentait de repousser mes oppresseurs et de me mettre à ma place."

Newtonian philosophers and their evil allies were con-
spiring against him in positions of power throughout
France: they were confiscating his books, conniving to
keep his letters out of journals, even plotting to suppress
his new truths in secret meetings of the faculty of medicine
(like the faculty's meetings to crush mesmerism). Marat's
desire to avenge himself against the Academy of Sciences
provided the main thrust behind his strange revolutionary
career, which was principally a campaign against con-
spirators. "One needs the zeal of a friend when one is
pitted against so powerful a faction," he confided to
Brissot in 1783. Mesmer was then fighting the same faction, and Marat probably sympathized with his parallel
struggle, although there is no evidence that Marat went
beyond his announcement in a letter to P.-R. Roume de
Saint Laurent of June 19, 1783: "I am going to look into
M. Mesmer and will send you a thorough report. But it
is no passing affair. You know how I like to examine
things and to examine them with care before pronouncing
on them." In any case, Brissot adopted Marat's views
of the conspiratorial academic establishment and sharp-
ened an attack on academic "despotism" in 1782 by
praising Marat for having "courageously overturned the
idol of the academic cult and substituted well-proved
facts for Newton's theory of light." Feeling himself barred
by the academic establishment from becoming a philosophe, Brissot, like Marat, threw himself into the revolutionary career that opened up for him in 1789. The
resentments produced by his frustrated literary and
scientific ambitions in the 1780's provided the crucial
element in that career, and probably in many careers
like his.[8]

8. Marat to Brissot, undated (1783), in Brissot's *Correspondance,*
p. 79; Marat to Roume de Saint Laurent, June 19, 1783, in A. Birembaut,
"Une lettre inédite de Marat à Roume," *Annales historiques de la Révolution Française* (1967), pp. 395–399; the final quotation is from Brissot,
De la vérité, pp. 173–174. Marat's letter to Roume should not be taken
as evidence that Marat believed in mesmerism, although Marat's

Mesmerism carried Brissot much further down the path of political radicalism than did Marat, for mesmerism provided him with a perfect anti-establishment cause, a cause, moreover, that had gripped and held the public's attention and that had united behind it the group of radicals who met at Kornmann's house and who offered to take in Brissot. Brissot accepted the invitation and threw himself into the movement by publishing another violent attack on academicians. "I have come to give you a lesson, gentlemen, and I have a right to do so; I am independent, and there is not one of you who is not a slave. I am not connected with any corps, and you are bound to yours. I don't cling to any prejudice, and you are chained by those of your corps; by those of all the persons in power whom you venerate basely as idols, although you secretly despise them."

In a letter to J. C. Lavater, the mesmerist-physiognomist-mystic, Brissot described the pamphlet containing this attack as "my profession of faith." Judging from the pamphlet itself, his faith was boundless, for Brissot declared his belief in the most extreme tenets of mesmerism with a spirit of indiscriminate credulity that

---

Mémoire sur l'électricité médicale . . . (Paris, 1784) shows that he refused to come out against it, and the mesmerists claimed that his experiments actually made the fluid visible (see J. B. Bonnefoy, *Analyse raisonnée des rapports des commissaires* . . . [Lyons, 1784], pp. 27–28). By 1791, Marat had relegated Mesmer to the class of "jongleurs," but he emphasized that academic "jalousie" accounted for the persecution of mesmerism, and he still fulminated against academic despotism (see Marat, *Les Charlatans modernes, ou lettres sur le charlatanisme académique* [Paris, 1791], pp. 6–7). The point is that his struggle against scientific officialdom paralleled Mesmer's. Marat best revealed his attitude to this struggle in his letters to Roume, especially the extraordinary letter of November 20, 1783, in *Correspondance de Marat, recueillie et annotée par Charles Vellay* (Paris, 1908), pp. 23–87. Marat's almost insane hatred of academicians should not obscure the fact that he was respected, if not lionized, as a scientist, even in 1785 (see *Journal de Physique,* September 1785, p. 237), nor the fact that he had reasons to fear a conspiracy against him. A police report, made between 1781 and 1785, stated, "M. Vicq d'Azir demande au nom de la Société Royale de Médecine qu'il [Marat] soit chassé de Paris" (Bibliothèque municipale, Orléans, ms 1423).

typified the occultism of his time: "An extraordinary fact is a fact that doesn't link up with those that we know or with laws that we have fabricated. But should we believe that we know all of them?" Never, he declared, had a discovery been so thoroughly proven as mesmerism, and he cited the works of Bergasse, Puységur, and Servan as evidence. He condemned the disdain of academicians for the mesmerist-tinged theories of Court de Gébelin, who "holds the common people, the downtrodden, close to his heart." He defended even those on the fringe of the movement, like Bléton, the water witcher, and Bottineau, the seer; and he championed the claims of somnambulists to perceive their own insides and to communicate with one another over great distances. In fact, Brissot revealed that he had shared such experiences himself. "But I, a father who fears doctors, I love mesmerism because it identifies me with my children. How sweet it is to me . . . when I see them obey my inner voice, bend over, fall into my arms and enjoy sleep! The state of a nursing mother is a state of perpetual mesmerism. We unfortunate fathers, caught up in our business affairs, we are practically nothing to our children. By mesmerism, we become fathers once again. Hence a new benefit for society, and it has such need of one!" If these allusions to breast feeding and family sentiment evoked Rousseau, it was because Brissot had read occult messages into Rousseau's works. In another pamphlet, his *Examen critique*, which announced his own perceptions of "sublime glimmers . . . beyond our globe, in a better world," he argued that to condemn illuminism was to condemn "almost all the true philosophers, and especially Rousseau. Read his Dialogues with himself. They seem written in another world. The author who exists only in this [world], who has never passed beyond its limits, could not write two sentences of them."

His Rousseauism inspired Brissot to see many implications, "even political, even moral," in mesmerist theory; so his mesmerist pamphlet proclaimed a new force for equality: "Don't you [academicians] see, for example, that mesmerism is a way to bring social classes closer together, to make the rich more humane, to make them into real fathers of the poor? Wouldn't you be edified at the sight of the most eminent men . . . supervising the health of their servants, spending hours at a time mesmerizing them?" But, Brissot noted pointedly, the academicians had "tried to inflame the government against the partisans of mesmerism"; and so he denounced their medico-politics: "I'm afraid that the habit of despotism has ossified your souls."

So violent were his denunciations that Brissot's defense of mesmerism seemed secondary to his desire to heap abuse on the "base parasites" and "oppressors of the fatherland" in the academies, on the "vile adulators" of the "magnates, of the rich, of princes" in the salons, and on the "half-talents who put themselves up front and drive true talent back into hiding." Brissot alluded to his own efforts to establish himself as a philosophic journalist in London, which had collapsed following his recent imprisonment in the Bastille. "If there is in your way one of these free, independent men . . . you praise him, you pity him, but you let it be known that his pen is dangerous, that the government has proscribed it, and that its proscription could bring about that of the journal." Academicians shut their doors to independent philosophers like the mesmerists, then inflamed the government against them. Only the courage of mesmerist leaders like Bergasse and d'Eprémesnil prevented them from being locked in prisons. And while the academicians suppressed Truth, they courted the fashionable public in organizations like La Harpe's Lyceum, where "for a sum you amuse stylish women [femmes de bon ton] and bored young men, who take a lesson in literature or history like a lesson in dancing or fencing." Brissot detested this alien world of bon ton. When he and his mesmerist friends threatened it, he found that it responded as it had always responded to innovation, reason, progress: by persecution. "It is here [concerning mesmerism] especially that you [academicians] have displayed your spirit of intrigue, your imperious despotism, your maneuvers among magnates and women." Brissot's mesmerism was a stage in the process of shifting his hatred of "nos aristocrates littéraires" (our literary aristocrats) to the aristocracy. By 1789 the struggle of the "independent" against the academic oligarchy had become absorbed in a more general fight for independence. This aspect of Brissot's radicalism has been misunderstood, because his biographers have been unable to find his mesmerist manifesto, appropriately entitled, *Un mot à l'oreille des académiciens de Paris*.[9]

As in Brissot's case, mesmerism gave Jean-Louis Carra a way of venting his fury at being excluded from his rightful place among the leading philosophers of Paris. Like Brissot, Carra laid claim to this place by publishing surveys and syntheses of vast domains of knowledge. He wrote a romantic novel, two metaphysical-ethical-political treatises, two books on Eastern Europe, a theoretical work on balloon flights, a six-volume translation of John Gillies' history of ancient Greece, and three abstruse works on physics and chemistry. In the popular scientific literature of the time one catches glimpses of him scrambling to advance himself—

9. Brissot's letter to Lavater, dated January 28, 1787, is in Zentralbibliothek, Zurich, Lavater papers, ms 149. The quotations come from J.-P. Brissot (anonymous), *Un mot à l'oreille des académiciens de Paris*, pp. 1, 3–10, 13, 15, 18, 20–21, 24; and Brissot, *Examen critique des Voyages dans l'Amérique Septentrionale de M. le Marquis de Chatellux . . .* (London, 1786), pp. 49, 55. The remark about literary aristocrats is on p. 21 of the *Examen.* I have found two copies of Brissot's *Mot* in the Bibliothèque historique de la ville de Paris. Brissot revealed the depth of his hatred of academicians and the "despotisme" of the fashionable salons from which he was excluded in *De la vérité*, p. 15, and esp. p. 319: "Ils me révoltaient, et je disais à ces tyrans dans la douleur de mon âme: vos cruautés ne seront pas toujours impunies: votre orgueil sera humilié: je ferai votre histoire, et vous serez couverts d'opprobre."

reading a comparison of "lucific" (lucifiques) and "conific" (conifiques) vibrations to the Museum of Court de Gébelin, for example, and publishing some experiments with sulphur in the *Journal de Paris*. He even managed to get a hearing from the Academy of Sciences for his proposal to steer balloons by applying an unintelligible geometric formula and rowing with taffeta "wings." But the academy refused to award him its special prize for the best project for directing balloons. The academy of Dijon also refused to take notice of his discovery that fire was produced by the "counter-shocks" of Marat's "igneous fluid" and Marivetz's mesmeric ether—not, Carra insisted, by the gases that Lavoisier had misunderstood so badly.

No one in respectable scientific circles seems to have taken Carra seriously, unless a stray word of praise in the *Journal des Sçavans*, which later closed its columns to him, was not meant to be ironic: "He is a creative genius; he explains everything down to the smell of a flower by centrifugal force." More typical was a letter in the *Courier de l'Europe* of January 17, 1783, by Joseph Lalande, the astronomer and academician. Carra had maligned the academies, Lalande maintained, because they had treated his works for what they were—"the absurdities and the dreaming of an imbecile." Carra responded to this treatment by adopting the pose of a misunderstood genius, a "prophète philosophe," who despised worldly success. "Except for a few men privileged by nature and by reason, the others are not made to understand me." But he destroyed the credibility of this pose by flying into a rage against the men at the top, especially nobles and kings, "monstrous crocodiles, vomiting flames on every side; their eyes are red with blood; they kill just by their look." This was hardly the tone of philosophic aloofness; it sounded more like the almost apoplectic declamations of Marat. Of course one cannot conclude from Carra's respectful references to Marat's scientific works that the two secluded themselves in the laboratory as if they were mad scientists sharing fantasies of blowing up the Ancien Régime with one of their wonderful fluids. But a mad, explosive atmosphere permeates their scientific treatises. For example, Carra prefaced a geological explanation of how the earth's poles would shift to the equator in 24,000 years with an appeal to the poor to demand their natural rights, to revolt against the rich, the nobles, and the kings, to "purge this very earth of the monsters that devour it."

His hatred of the established order festered deep within him, for the forces of that order had smashed into his life and carried him away to prison at the age of sixteen under suspicion of being a thief. At about this time his mother died. His father had died when he was seven. So in prison he may well have felt cut off from everything, from family, friends, and the sort of career that awaited his schoolmates who continued their Latin, rhetoric, and philosophy under the good Jesuits of Mâcon. Young Carra must have philosophized in a different manner in his prison; and he had time to think, because he remained there for two years and four months. After his release, he wandered through Germany and the Balkans, supporting himself by hack writing and whatever else came to hand. By the time Mesmer began to battle the scientific establishment, Carra had settled in Paris as an employe in the Bibliothèque du Roi, a self-proclaimed successor of Newton, and, like Marat and Brissot, a professional outsider. From Carra's point of view, mesmerism looked like a revolutionary cause; and, indeed, it led him into the Revolution, where he at last found an outlet for his pent-up hatreds as a politician, journalist, and supporter of Brissot, his former mesmerist companion in the Kornmann group.[10]

10. Among Carra's works, see esp. *Nouveaux principes de physique*, 3 vols. (Paris, 1781–1782); *Système de la raison ou le prophète philosophe* (London, 1782); *Esprit de la morale et de la philosophie* (The Hague, 1777); *Dissertation élémentaire sur la nature de la lumière, de la chaleur, du feu*

Nicolas Bergasse shared the disgust of Brissot and Carra at the closed, aristocratic character of the Parisian world of letters, but he had more in common with Brissot's broader demand "to open up to merit the path to dignities, to honors." "What a source of power is ambition! Happy is the state, where, in order to be first, it is necessary only to be greatest in merit." Again and again, Bergasse sounded the same theme, which he developed most fully in his *Observations sur le préjugé de la noblesse héréditaire:* "Our liberty must be given back to us; all careers must be opened up to us." The theme came more naturally to Bergasse than to Brissot, for Brissot teetered on the brink of bankruptcy before the Revolution, while Bergasse enjoyed a considerable income from his family's businesses. Bergasse's father had married into a prominent commercial family of Lyons and had gone into commerce himself in the 1740's. Nicolas' four brothers became wealthy merchants, and Nicolas always main-

---

et de l'électricité (London, 1787), based partly on the mesmerist experiments he described in the *Journal de Paris,* May 11, 1784, pp. 572–573; *Essai sur la nautique aérienne . . .* (1784); and *Examen physique du magnétisme animal . . .* (London, 1785). The quotations come from Carra's *Dissertation,* p. 28 (the Baron de Marivetz, a member of the Société de l'Harmonie of Paris and a friend of Brissot's, developed an anti-Newtonian ether theory in his popular *Physique du Monde* [1780–1787]); *Journal des Sçavans,* February 1784, pp. 111–112; Carra (anonymously), *Système de la raison,* pp. 151, 52, 68. Carra set the passionate tone of this book by his opening challenge "aux prétendus maîtres de la terre" (p. 5): "Fléaux du genre humain, illustres tyrans de vos semblables, hommes qui n'avez que le titre, rois, princes, monarques, empereurs, chefs, souverains, vous tous enfin qui, en vous élevant sur le trône et au-dessus de vos semblables, avez perdu les idées d'égalité, d'équité, de sociabilité . . . je vous assigne au tribunal de la raison." The only sketch of his obscure early career is P. Montarlot, "Carra," from "Les députés de Saône-et-Loire aux Assemblées de la Révolution," in *Mémoires de la Société Eduenne* (1905), new series, XXXIII, 217–224. See also Appendix 2. Two letters from Carra to the Société Typographique de Neuchâtel, dated December 6 and 21, 1771, exist in the society's manuscripts in the Archives de la ville de Neuchâtel, ms 1131. They provide evidence of his vitriolic temperament but do not tell much about his career, aside from his quarrel with his employer, L. C. Gaudot, of the *Supplément* to the *Encyclopédie.*

tained an interest in commercial affairs, but preferred to teach in Oratorian schools, then to qualify for the bar, and finally to philosophize privately while nursing his ill health. "My wealth is generally known; it is no secret that it more than provides for my needs, that it makes me absolutely independent," he wrote in 1789, and he outlined this fortune in a letter to his fiancée, Perpétue du Petit-Thouars, in December 1790: "Before it pleased this good people to want to be free, I had a capital that brought me five to six thousand livres in income and in addition a share in my brothers' company that brought me ten thousand livres annually and later was to bring me more." Bergasse represented the commercial bourgeois who welcomed the calling of the Estates General as a means of winning a political role commensurate with their economic importance. He developed this view in some of the most important of the pamphlets about the composition of the Estates General in 1789. Denouncing the aristocracy's dominance in the church, the army, and the judiciary as well as in the academies, he derided the absurdity of privilege based upon birth, the nobles' origin in "the sad chaos of feudal government," and their inability to perform successfully in the posts reserved so unjustly for them. He had emphasized the bourgeois character of his demands nine years earlier in an essay calling for free trade in the name of "the industrious class of the nation." The essay distinguished neatly between this class, composed mainly of merchants and landowners like the Bergasses, and "that class of the common people that has no property."[11]

11. J.-P. Brissot, *Un indépendant à l'ordre des avocats*, pp. 47–48; Nicolas Bergasse, *Observations sur le préjugé de la noblesse héréditaire* (London, 1789), pp. 40 and 5; Bergasse, *Observations du sieur Bergasse dans la cause du sieur Kornmann* (1789), p. 7; Bergasse's letter to Perpétue, not dated exactly, is in his papers at the Château de Villiers, Villiers, Loir-et-Cher. The letter explained that his two brothers in Lyons had 500,000 livres in capital, which they expected to double in ten years, and his two brothers in Marseilles, though less wealthy, were well off. In a letter to Perpétue dated May 7 (1789?) he described their practice

Bergasse first developed his anti-aristocratic ideas in notes to a mesmerist pamphlet, *Autres rêveries sur le magnétisme animal,* by his friend and convert to mesmerism, the Abbé Petiot, who was a secretary of the Society of Harmony. The pamphlet denounced the "scientific intolerance" of academicians and drew this conclusion from their attacks on mesmerism: "In general, all exclusive privileges are favorable to some sort of aristocracy; only the king and the people have a constant common interest." This defense of mesmerism anticipated the main thrust of radical propaganda of 1789: the king and the third estate should ally against the aristocracy. Bergasse made this position perfectly clear in his notes, which shifted the argument against the academies' privileges to a broad attack on all privileges derived from "feudal anarchy." He heaped scorn upon everything connected with the aristocracy—its heraldry, its pomp, its claim to privileges because of its ancestry, its "chivalric superstition." Indignant at the feudal reaction that was then animating the aristocracy, he protested, "One must be born before the fourteenth century to pretend to maintain near the throne an aristocratic system that determines the order in which the king must choose those serving him in his household and his army." The bourgeois should oppose the noble's claims to traditional privileges by replying that "he does not know how to read Gothic." Bergasse demanded the opening of all top posts to the third estate and warned it to beware of collusion between the two privileged orders, "which

---

of sharing profits, "l'espèce de système républicain qui existe entre nous, comment toutes nos richesses sont communes, l'un ne voulant jamais être plus fortuné que l'autre." The final two quotations come from Bergasse, *Considérations sur la liberté du commerce . . .* (The Hague, 1780), pp. 61–62. The main study of Bergasse, the "monarchien" whose disaffection with the Revolution has obscured his role as a leading radical from 1787 until October 1789, is the biography written anonymously by his descendant, Louis Bergasse, *Un défenseur des principes traditionnels sous la Révolution, Nicolas Bergasse* (Paris, 1910).

keep two votes for the same purpose" (qui conserve deux voix pour le même voeu). He called upon the people to unite with the king "in order to make all citizens noble and all nobles citizens." He formulated the great question that was to be repeated endlessly in the pamphleteering of 1789: "How do you hope to succeed in your attempt to strip the ancient aristocracy of its influence, which is more lucrative than its antiquated power?" And he answered it, "You will have for you only the law, the people and the King." No less extreme than the classic formulation of the third estate's demands by Siéyès in 1789, this appeal appeared in a mesmerist pamphlet of 1784 that was ostensibly intended to refute the royal commission's report against animal magnetism.[12]

At this point it should be clear that an underground current of radicalism ran throughout the mesmerist movement and occasionally erupted in violent political pamphlets. Mesmerism offered Brissot, Carra, and Bergasse an opportunity to declaim against abuses that seemed to impede their advancement and that of their class. Some of their mesmerist colleagues, however— notably Lafayette, Duport, and d'Eprémesnil—enjoyed very exalted positions in the Ancien Régime. Lafayette and Duport used their positions to lead the revolutionary cause from 1787 to 1789, but d'Eprémesnil has been cast

12. *Autres rêveries sur le magnétisme animal, à un académicien de province* (Brussels, 1784), quotations from pp. 21, 39, 46–47. A very accurate contemporary work on mesmerism in Paris (*Testament politique de M. Mesmer* . . . [Leipzig, 1785; by a Dr. Bruck, according to A.-A. Barbier], p. 32) said this pamphlet was written by Petiot and "corrigé et noté" by Bergasse (the notes were longer than the text). It was a sequel to Petiot's *Lettre de M. l'abbé Pxxx de l'Académie de la Rochelle à Mxxx de la même académie* (1784), which eulogized Bergasse. Petiot also wrote a violent attack on academicians and aristocrats in 1789, *La liberté de la presse, dénonciation d'une nouvelle conspiration de l'aristocratie française* . . . The only information on Petiot's obscure career is a brief manuscript notice in the Bibliothèque municipale de la Rochelle, ms 358. In *Le Patriote françois* of March 16, 1791, Brissot wrote, "M. l'abbé Petiot professait ouvertement dans Paris, depuis dix ans, la doctrine anti-aristocratique."

by historians in the role of a reactionary. In fact, many historians regard d'Eprémesnil as the leader of the aristocratic revolt of 1787–1788 that precipitated the Revolution. The ambiguities of the "révolte nobiliaire" thesis lie beyond the range of this study, but the ambiguous role of d'Eprémesnil is relevant in reconstructing the contemporary view of events. Few Frenchmen considered d'Eprémesnil or the Parlement of Paris reactionary before September 25, 1788, the date of the Parlement's recommendation that the Estates General be organized in a way that favored the aristocracy. If the bookseller S.-P. Hardy represents the views of a typical Parisian bourgeois, d'Eprémesnil was seen as a "humane, charitable magistrate," a popular hero who dared "repulse the attacks against the citizens' liberty," a martyred "patriot," "forever famous" for being imprisoned in June 1788 as a result of the "cruel persecution on the part of the ministers." This view may have been wrong, but it existed and exerted an important influence on events in the summer of 1788. The loathsome sight of the Bastille probably hid the aristocratic revolt from the eyes of most Parisians at that time. In any case, there was nothing incongruous in the alliance in Kornmann's house of members of Parlement like d'Eprémesnil and Duport and hack pamphleteers like Brissot and Carra, and there was nothing that their contemporaries or they themselves would have recognized as reactionary in their attacks on the government or in their mesmeric theory of revolution.[13]

13. The quotations are from Hardy's journal in the Bibliothèque Nationale, fonds français, 6687, entries for October 1, 1787, and May 5, 6, and 18, 1788. The only special study on d'Eprémesnil is Henri Carré, "Un précurseur inconscient de la Révolution: le conseiller Duval d'Eprémesnil (1787–1788)," *La Révolution Française,* October and November 1897, pp. 349–373 and 405–437. Lenoir believed that d'Eprémesnil's house was a center of sedition (Bibliothèque municipale, Orléans, ms 1423). The "Révolte nobiliaire" thesis is best known in this country from Georges Lefebvre's *Quatre-vingt-neuf,* translated by R. R. Palmer as *The Coming of the French Revolution: 1789* (Princeton, 1947).

4. MESMERISM AS A RADICAL POLITICAL THEORY

Mesmerism provided embittered hack writers like Carra with a weapon against the exclusive scientific and literary bodies of Paris, but it presented itself to most readers as a scientific cosmology. Carra and his friends, especially Bergasse, dealt with the cosmological side of mesmerism by extracting a political theory from the obscure, strictly apolitical pontifications of Mesmer. "Political theory" may be too dignified a term for their distortions of his ideas, but they themselves considered their theories consistent and reasonable, and the police viewed them as a threat to the state. Just how political the mesmerist sessions became is difficult to tell because there is no record of the discussions that went on in Kornmann's house. Also, the censors and the police forced the radical mesmerists to be cautious in their publications; so it is only by piecing together remarks scattered throughout their printed works that one can reconstruct their political ideas.

Carra's ideology exemplifies the Kornmann group's attempt to divorce mesmerism from Mesmer, but it really owed much to the master. Carra even provided for the tub and for "chain" mesmerizing, although he disputed Mesmer's understanding of the fluid. Carra's conception of the fluid derived from a dissenting report, somewhat in favor of mesmerism, by A. L. Jussieu, one of the commissioners of the Royal Society of Medicine. Jussieu attributed the effects of mesmerizing in part to the "atmospheres" surrounding bodies, and Carra incorporated this interpretation into his own mesmerist cosmology by positing the existence of interrelated fluids, which penetrated the atmospheres of all persons and substances. He put these fluids to work, providing air, light, heat, electricity, and fire (all of which he explained by new theories) and associated them with a general fluid, like Mesmer's, which acted as an intermediary between a universal ether and the particular atmosphere of all bodies, large and small.

Obscure as it was, Carra's atmosphere theory provided him with a seemingly scientific approach to politics. Moral causes, like unjust legislation, disrupted one's atmosphere and hence one's health, just as physical causes produced sickness; and conversely, physical causes could produce moral effects, even on a broad scale. "The same effects take place, every moment, in society; and one has not yet ventured to acknowledge their importance, I believe, because one has not yet sufficiently connected the moral to the physical." During the Revolution, Carra traced his republican political views to a prophecy in his *Nouveaux principes de physique* (1781–1782) that France would become a republic, "because the great physical system of the universe, which governs the moral and political affairs of the human race, is itself a veritable republic." By 1787 he unhesitatingly linked virtue and vice with the "mechanism of the universe" (see p. 19), and he considered politics and medicine to be so intimately related that both physical and social ills could be cured by a combination of cold baths, head-washing, dieting, and philosophical books. He claimed that ancient prophets and wizards practiced a primitive mesmerism and that the Delphic Oracle's predictions and support of Lycurgus' legislation were a form of political somnambulism.

Carra generally restricted his main mesmerist work, *Examen physique du magnétisme animal* (1785), to theorizing about atmospheric fluids, but he indicated the political side to his theories by announcing that mesmerism had helped inaugurate the third of the three stages in history that he had outlined in his *Esprit de la morale*

Nicolas Bergasse, Mesmer's most energetic disciple and propagandist. Bergasse lectured on mesmerist theory to neophytes in the Society of Universal Harmony. After a split in the society, he led the group of radicals who saw a Rousseauist political message in mesmerism.

Nicolas Bergasse
1750   1832

et de la philosophie (1777). In this anonymous work, Carra declaimed against nobles and kings and hailed the outbreak of the American Revolution as a victory for Rousseau's principle of popular sovereignty. He prophesied that this principle would rule the world in the third and final stage of history, the stage of "positive natural right" (droit naturel positif), which he described in a parable about a king and a shepherd on a desert island. "The one is no longer a king; the other is always a shepherd; or rather they are no longer anything but two men in the true state of equality, two friends in the true state of society. The political difference has disappeared . . . Nature, equality, have reclaimed all their rights . . . It is up to you, my fellow men, my brothers, to direct the working of your particular will according to this model, in order to coordinate it with the production of the general good." Carra believed that the physico-moral forces of the universe would bring about this revolution, and by 1785 he was convinced that they had begun their work. He detected an impending apocalypse in the extraordinary weather of the mid-1780's. Heavy fogs, an earthquake, and a volcanic eruption had disturbed various parts of Europe in the summer of 1783; the winter of 1783–84 was extremely severe (the *Journal de Physique* reported below-freezing temperatures for 69 days and numerous deaths from exposure and marauding wolves), and it was followed by catastrophic floods during the spring. This was enough for Carra; he announced the imminent outbreak of the mesmerist revolution in 1785. "The entire globe seems to be preparing itself, by a pronounced upheaval in the course of the seasons, for physical changes . . . In societies the masses are agitating more than ever to disentangle at last the chaos of their morals and their legislation." Carra's mesmerist ideas hardly added up to a coherent philosophy, but they illustrate the curious combination of scientific and polit-

ical extremism that went into the making of several
revolutionaries.[1]

Other radical mesmerists certainly held similar ideas.
Adrien Duport, for example, mixed physics, occultism,
and politics in his mesmerist theories, according to the
Abbé Siéyès. "He pretended then to elevate the doctrine
of animal magnetism to the highest degree of illumination; he saw everything in it: medicine, ethics, political
economy, philosophy, astronomy, the past, the present
at all distances and even the future; all this filled only a
small part of his vast mesmeric vision."[2] The Rolands and
their future Girondist colleague François Lanthenas went
through a mesmerist phase before the Revolution. Although nothing indicates they associated mesmerism
with political theory, they may have shared the belief
expressed by their friend Brissot in 1791: "Liberty . . . is
the principle of health." Impressed by the healthiness of
the Americans he had met during a trip to the United
States in 1788, Brissot jumped to a typically extravagant
conclusion. "There will, no doubt, come a day when one

1. Jussieu published his findings separately as *Rapport de l'un des
commissaires chargés par le Roi de l'examen du magnétisme animal* (Paris,
1784). The quotations come from Carra's *Examen physique du magnétisme
animal* . . . (London, 1785), pp. 80–81; *Précis de défense de Carra* . . .
(Year II), p. 49; *Histoire de l'ancienne Grèce* . . . (Paris, 1787–1788; this is
Carra's six-volume translation of John Gillies' history, to which he
added extensive notes on anything that interested him—thus the
"mécanisme de l'univers," II, 471, and the analysis of the Delphic
Oracle, I, 176); *Système de la raison* . . . (London, 1782), p. 35 (his prescription for social-physical ills is on p. 124, and related declamations
are on pp. 56–68, 177, 220–224); the final quotation is from his *Examen
physique*, p. 3. Carra was skeptical, however, about Bergasse's claim
that mesmerism could produce drastic political reforms (*ibid.*, p. 8),
as he believed they would come from physical causes like seasonal and
astronomical influences. For attitudes toward the unusual weather of the
mid-1780's, see *Journal de Physique*, December 1784, pp. 455–466; *Journal
de Bruxelles*, June 19, 1784, pp. 125–133; and *Journal de Paris*, April 6,
1784, pp. 428–429, which explained that the unequal distribution of
the electric and phlogistic fluids had prepared "la convulsion du globe."

2. Abbé Siéyès, *Notice sur la vie de Siéyès* . . . (Switzerland, 1795),
pp. 15–16.

will be convinced that the great principle of physical
health is the equality of all beings and the independence
of opinions and wills." But Brissot never incorporated
mesmerism into a systematic political theory. The only
mesmerist theoretician who left a thorough record of
his ideas was Nicolas Bergasse, Mesmer's high priest
before the founding of the Kornmann group. It was
Bergasse, not Mesmer, who lectured to neophytes in the
Society of Harmony; Bergasse wrote a textbook for them
to study; he composed statements of dogma to refute
schismatics in Mesmer's name; and he published the
mesmerist *Summa Theologica,* his *Considérations sur le
magnétisme animal* (1784). One must turn to Bergasse's
works, therefore, for the most important political version
of mesmerism, assuming that Bergasse's friends agreed
with him in a general way, as Brissot indicated in his
attack on academicians: "When the most fervent apostle
of mesmerism, M. Bergasse, pulverized your report in
his profound Considérations, you said, 'He is strong-minded
but too enthusiastic.'" Brissot denounced the academicians for attempting to "crush the man with an independent spirit. But one praises such a man by describing him
in this way, for to say that a man is enthusiastic is to say
that his ideas fly beyond the range of ordinary ideas,
that he has civic virtues under a corrupt government,
charity among barbarians, respect for the rights of man
under despotism . . . And this, in truth, is the portrait
of M. Bergasse."[3]

Like Carra, Bergasse built his mesmerist system on
the popular contemporary theory of reciprocal moral and
physical causality, which formed a central theme in many

3. On the mesmerism of Lanthenas and the Rolands, see the letters
of Mme. Roland to her husband of May 10–15, 16, and 21, 1784, in
Lettres de Madame Roland, ed. Claude Perroud (Paris, 1900–1902), I,
405–406, 408, and 427. The quotations are from J.-P. Brissot, *Nouveau
voyage dans les Etats-Unis de l'Amérique septentrionale, fait en 1788* (Paris,
1791), II, 143 and 133–134; J.-P. Brissot, *Un mot à l'oreille des académiciens
de Paris,* p. 14.

mesmerist writings, particularly after the report of the royal commission. The report had discredited mesmerism by attributing its physical effects, such as convulsions, to a "moral" faculty, the imagination, and Bailly had told the Academy of Sciences that the commission's investigation had promoted "a new science, that of the influence of the moral on the physical." Mesmerists turned Bailly's analysis against him by hailing animal magnetism as this very new science. Antoine Servan rejoiced, "What! those physical and moral phenomena that I admire every day without understanding are caused by the same agent . . ." and concluded, "All beings are therefore my brothers, and nature is simply our common mother!"[4]

Bergasse agreed that nature governed both the moral and physical worlds, because he believed that mesmerist fluid—"the conservative action of nature" (l'action conservatrice de la nature)—operated as both a physical and moral force. He developed this idea by drawing on contemporary concepts of natural law as both a physical and normative order. In two mesmerist lectures that have survived in his papers, he explained that nature intended her laws to maintain "a constant and durable harmony," the natural state of the fluid in regulating relations among inanimate bodies and among men. Disharmony, or sickness, had moral as well as physical

4. J.-S. Bailly, *Exposé des expériences qui ont été faites pour l'examen du magnétisme animal . . .* (1784), quotation from p. 11; (Bailly), *Rapport des commissaires chargés par le Roi de l'examen du magnétisme animal* (Paris, 1784), esp. p. 48; A.-J.-M. Servan, *Doutes d'un provincial . . .* (Lyons, 1784), pp. 82–83. Court de Gébelin also exulted to learn from Mesmer that "la Nature . . . opérait dans le moral de la même manière que dans le physique" (*Lettre de l'auteur du Monde Primitif . . .* [Paris, 1784], p. 16). See also Pierre Thouvenel, *Mémoire physique et médicinal . . .* (London, 1784), p. 34, and Charles Deslon, *Observations sur les deux rapports de MM. les commissaires . . .* (1784), p. 20. An example of the common theorizing about moral and physical causality in the eighteenth century is Montesquieu's *Essai sur les causes,* an important source for *De l'esprit des lois* (see Robert Shackleton, *Montesquieu: A Critical Biography* [Oxford, 1961], pp. 314–319).

causes; indeed, virtue was a necessity for good health, and even wicked thoughts could make one ill. The conscience was a physical organ "that is united by numerous, slender threads to all points in the universe . . . It is by this organ that we put ourselves in harmony with nature." Good was harmony, evil disharmony in both a physical and moral sense, for Bergasse had found in mesmerism "a morality issuing from the world's general physics" (une morale émanée de la physique générale du monde). He adopted terms like "artificial moral magnetism" and "artificial moral electricity" to describe the physico-moral forces that operated in society and in politics as well as within individuals and among planets. The peaceful flow of the fluid would produce a blissfully healthy, happy, and justly organized France. Bergasse told the members of the Society of Harmony, whose name suggested this ideal, that mesmerism provided "simple rules for judging the institutions to which we are enslaved, certain principles for establishing the legislation appropriate for man in all given circumstances." The Societies of Harmony devoted themselves to the "contemplation of the harmony of the universe" and the "knowledge of the laws of nature." Their emblem elaborated their parallel physical and moral objectives (for example, "universal physics" and "universal justice") and pledged the societies to perform parallel practical activities—to mesmerize the sick back to health and also to "prevent injustice." It listed "social virtues" of a bourgeois nature ("frugality," "honesty," and "correctness in conduct"), and it advocated the natural rights of man, "security, liberty, property."[5]

Bergasse used his concept of natural law as a means of criticizing French society but not of edging God out

5. Bergasse's lectures, part of which are printed in Appendix 4, are in his manuscripts at the Château de Villiers, Villiers, Loir-et-Cher. The society's emblem is reproduced in Appendix 5.

of the cosmos; far from it, he felt compelled to attribute the omnipresent fluid's action to a divine intelligence. "Nothing better agrees with the notions we have formed of a Supreme Being, nothing proves more his profound wisdom, than the idea of the world being formed as the result of a single idea, moved by a single law." This common argument for theism from design owed something to Descartes, despite the Newtonian pose of most mesmerist writing. In fact, some mesmerists criticized Newton for rejecting Descartes' "subtle matter," which they interpreted as an interplanetary mesmeric fluid, and they contradicted Newton's version of gravity by proclaiming, "Gravity is an occult virtue, a property inhering, no one knows how, in matter." Bergasse began his secret notebook for neophytes with a Cartesian formula: "There exists one uncreated principle: God. There exist in Nature two created principles: matter and movement." This credo, which was reproduced in many mesmerist works, is interesting because it was written in symbols instead of words. Mesmerists regarded the notebook as "a book of doctrine written in mystical characters." Its cabalistic signs communicated meaning beyond the reach of words; they transmitted the pure doctrine as Mesmer had received it from Nature during a three-month retreat in the wilderness. "Animal magnetism, in M. Mesmer's hands, seems to be nothing other than Nature herself," Deslon observed. Another mesmerist called it "the demonstrated presence of God," and in reproducing Bergasse's credo, he proclaimed the magic power of the number three and drew a triangle with the word "Dieu" at the top and "la matière" and "le mouvement" at the sides. This belief in the occult power of symbols and numbers derived from the vogue of illuminism and religious mysticism, which apparently represented a reaction during the last years of the Ancien Régime against the colder, sometimes atheistic rationalism of the earlier part of the century. In 1786 the Society of Harmony required its members to swear belief in God and the immortality of the soul, and it excluded "creatures so deprived of sense as to be materialists." Corberon remarked in his notes on a lecture by Bergasse, "It follows from this that movement is communicated by God, which is incontestable and an answer equally simple and strong to atheism."[6]

The mesmerists' mystical idea of nature evoked Rousseau, particularly as they often contrasted primitive nature with the decadence of modern society. They sometimes maintained that mesmerism offered a return to the "natural" medicine of Hippocrates or to the science of some forgotten primitive people. This theory especially pleased the followers of Court de Gébelin, the philosopher who searched ancient languages for traces of a lost primitive science. Gébelin himself adopted it in a letter he sent to his subscribers in place of the ninth volume of his *Monde primitif* in 1783. In the course of an impassioned defense of animal magnetism, he announced that Mesmer had helped him recover both his shattered health and the trail of his primitive science, which was a form of mesmerism. Gébelin joined the Society of Harmony,

6. Nicolas Bergasse, *Considérations sur le magnétisme animal* (The Hague, 1784), p. 43; Galart de Montjoie, *Lettre sur le magnétisme animal* . . . (Paris, 1784), p. 25; *Système raisonné du magnétisme universel* . . . (1786), pp. iii, 110, 121; Charles Deslon, *Observations sur le magnétisme animal* (London, 1784), p. 101; *Nouvelle découverte sur le magnétisme animal* . . . , pp. 1, 14; Corberon's journal, Bibliothèque municipale, Avignon, ms 3059, entry for April 7, 1784. Bergasse's notebook, entitled *Théorie du monde et des êtres organisés,* with a key for decoding it, is in the Bibliothèque Nationale, 4° Tb 62.1 (17); a sample page is reproduced in Appendix 5. It was reprinted in modified form by Caullet de Veaumorel as *Aphorismes de M. Mesmer* . . . (1785). Several mesmerists testified to Bergasse's authorship of the notebook, including Bergasse himself: *Observations de M. Bergasse sur un écrit du Docteur Mesmer* . . . (London, 1785), p. 25. On the persistent Cartesian strain in French eighteenth-century science, see Aram Vartanian, *Diderot and Descartes: A Study of Scientific Naturalism in the Enlightenment* (Princeton, 1953).

moved into the Hôtel de Coigny with Mesmer, and became one of his most effective proselytizers—until he
died at a mesmerist tub a year later. Mesmer himself
presented his theory as "the remnant of a primitively
recognized truth," which he had discovered in an attempt
to commune with nature by fleeing society. He had
wandered alone in a forest for three months like a Rous-
seauite savage: "I felt closer to nature there . . . O nature,
I cried out in those paroxysms, what do you want of me?"
In this inspired state, he had managed to erase from his
mind all ideas acquired from society, to think without
using words (which Rousseau had shown to be social
artifices), and to imbibe the pure philosophy of nature.
He had arrived in Paris like a natural man, stupefied
at the prejudices of civilization, and had vowed to "pass
on to humanity, in all the purity that I had received from
Nature, the inestimable benefaction that I had in hand."[7]

The correlation between the ideas of Gébelin and
Mesmer indicates the way in which Bergasse applied this
philosophy of nature. He attacked the moral and political
standards of his time by contrasting modern depravity
with primitive virtue and health. This technique also
suggested Rousseau's condemnation of modern society,
as the Abbé le Gros emphasized in a book comparing the
works of Rousseau and Gébelin. "They endlessly insisted
upon the happiness of the earliest ages, upon the prejudices, the corruption of the present time, upon the necessity of a revolution, of a general reform." Bergasse not
only read and admired Rousseau; he sought him out in

7. Elie de la Poterie, *Examen de la doctrine d'Hippocrate* . . . (Brest,
1785); *De la philosophie corpusculaire* . . . (Paris, 1785); Court de Gébelin,
Lettre de l'auteur du Monde Primitif; F. A. Mesmer, *Précis historique des
faits relatifs au magnétisme animal* . . . (London, 1781), pp. 20–25. Another
mesmerist extolled "l'ignorance primitive" and advocated mesmerism
as a means of returning to "l'état pur de la nature" and escaping from
"le torrent des institutions sociales" (*Nouvelle découverte sur le magnétisme animal*, pp. 4–5).

person and directed their conversation toward a favorite subject. "Our talk was more solemn when he threw himself into a discussion of morality and of the present constitution of governments . . . We are on the brink of a great revolution, he added." Bergasse even considered himself a kind of mesmerist Rousseau, as he indicated in a letter to his fiancée, Perpétue du Petit-Thouars: "You are not the first who has noted some resemblance between me and your good friend Jean-Jacques. However, there are some principles that he did not know and that would have made him less unhappy." Unlike the other Frenchmen who identified themselves with Jean-Jacques after tearful readings of *La Nouvelle Héloïse* or the *Confessions,* Bergasse incorporated Rousseau's disparate ideas into a system, and so retained the moral fervor of the master while abandoning some of his awkward axioms, like the contractual origin of society. Bergasse believed that man was a naturally social creature and that a truly natural and primitive society must have been created coevally with man. Primitive society, like the original cosmos, was a divine creation ruled by perfect harmony; it was a normative order to which France should return. "The word society must not be taken to mean society as it exists now . . . but the society that ought to exist, natural society, the one that results from the relations that our own natures, when well ordered, must produce . . . The guiding rule of society is harmony." Bailly later recalled that when he and Bergasse tried to prepare a constitution for revolutionary France in the Constitutional Committee of the National Assembly, "M. Bergasse, in order to speak of the constitution and of the rights of man, made us go back to the rule of Nature, to the state of savagery."[8]

8. Abbé Le Gros, *Analyse des ouvrages de J.-J. Rousseau de Genève et de M. Court de Gébelin, auteur du Monde Primitif* (Geneva and Paris, 1785), p. 5; letter from Bergasse to his friend Rambaud de Vallières, cited in Louis Bergasse, *Un défenseur des principes traditionnels sous*

Having defined his ideal of primitive, harmonious society, Bergasse searched in mesmerist doctrine for the means of restoring it; and like Rousseau, he came up with a theory of education, which also served as a weapon for attacking contemporary society. Bergasse felt that Rousseau had pointed the way to an educational theory that would regenerate society. Jean-Jacques had rightly stressed the interaction of physical and moral forces upon children's development, but he had lacked the key to the understanding of these forces—mesmerism. Bergasse showed that the action of mesmerist fluid determined the development of children in two ways: through the direct influence of other beings, and indirectly through the transmission of sensations from which children built ideas.

Bergasse explained that all bodies, men and planets alike, influenced each other by setting the fluid in motion. The more regular and powerful influence of the planets provided him with a scientific version of astrology, and the variable influences among men suggested a scientific explanation of Rousseau's theory of pity or empathy, the basis of the social virtues. One could not control the effect of the stars upon a child (although Mesmer later claimed to have mesmerized the sun), but one could surround him with the right sort of people. These would have constitutions with which he could empathize; that is, their fluid would flow evenly into him, communicating their health

la Révolution, Nicolas Bergasse (Paris, 1910), p. 24; letter from Bergasse to Perpétue du Petit-Thouars, dated "ce 21" (1791?), in his papers at Villiers; Bergasse's notebook, Théorie du Monde, "troisième partie." On his disagreement with the contract theory, see Bergasse, Mémoire sur une question d'adultère . . . (1787), pp. 75–76, 80. Bergasse, Brissot, and Carra knew and admired Gébelin and cited his Monde Primitif . . . (Paris, 1787–1789; 1 ed., 1773–1782), which contains some strong political views, in spite of its royal backing (e.g., Gébelin's remark on "l'harmonie primitive" in I, 87, and his "Vue générale" in VIII). Bailly's remark is in Mémoires de Bailly . . . ed. S. A. Berville and Barrière (Paris, 1821), I, 299.

and virtue, destroying all obstacles to harmony. This theory also held hope for treating sick and wicked adults, for mesmerists cured all forms of degeneration by placing themselves "en rapport" with a patient and subjecting him to the forceful flow of their salubrious fluid. Since "morals [les moeurs] in general result from the relations among men," such treatment promised the ultimate moral regeneration of the nation. "Any change, any alteration of our physical constitution thus produces infallibly a change, an alteration in our moral constitution. Therefore, it suffices to purify or corrupt the physical order of things in a nation in order to produce a revolution in its morals." As "morals are the cement of the political edifice," this moral revolution would transform political institutions.[9]

A vivid sense of the obstacles to harmony within France prevented Bergasse from expecting a quick arrival of the mesmerist millennium. He recommended that mesmerists concentrate on developing virtues in children, whose minds had not been completely scarred by a depraved society. As a good empiricist, Rousseau had shown that children's moral development depended upon the sensations they received, but he had not known the crucial truth revealed by mesmerism—that sensations were transmitted by means of Mesmer's all-purpose fluid. This truth provided a scientific basis for Rousseau's theory about the pernicious effects of the arts. Man enjoyed good health and morals in natural society because his primitive arts did not present too many sensations to his "sensibility." His moral decline began at the

---

9. Bergasse, *Considérations*, pp. 78–79, 84; Bergasse, *Lettre d'un médecin de la faculté de Paris* . . . (The Hague, 1781), p. 54. These two works, along with Bergasse's notebook, *Théorie du monde*, and his *Dialogue entre un docteur . . . et un homme de bon sens* . . . (1784), as well as his papers in Villiers, supply the basis for this discussion of his mesmerist theories.

point where his organs became damaged by registering the jarring impressions of highly developed arts. Luxury, gluttony, debauchery, the whole gamut of sensations offered by the modern French way of life had produced disharmony in men and corrupted their morals. Moreover, political institutions buttressed this way of life, and so "we owe almost all the physical ailments that consume us to our institutions." Bergasse projected a reformation of the arts, but he subordinated this task to the more pressing need of regenerating French morals and politics.[10]

"We have lost almost all connection with nature," Bergasse wailed in a declamation against the arts, morals, and politics of modern France. "The child born today, whose constitution has been modified by the customs . . . of society throughout several centuries, always must carry within him seeds of depravity, whether considerable or not." This depravity had eaten away the natural physico-moral strength of the classes most exposed to the arts and artificiality of civilization. The common people, however, retained some of their primitive virtue and were therefore healthier and easier to cure when sick. A vaguely democratic tone existed in the call Bergasse issued in Mesmer's name to mobilize the virtue of peasants and country curates: "It is especially in the country and in the most indigent and least depraved class of society that my discovery will bear fruit. It is easy there to place man again under the rule of Nature's conservative laws." And Bergasse repeated in his *Considérations,* "The common man, the man who lives in the fields, recovers quicker and better, when he is sick, than the worldly man." Bergasse believed that the more civilized classes lived in such an advanced stage of depravity that their children could not regain health and virtue as the

10. Quotation from *Lettre d'un médecin,* p. 51.

peasants did, merely by being exposed to nature. It was necessary to "double . . . the energy of nature herself" by mesmerizing. Mesmer cured Kornmann's son of partial blindness by making him spend hours at the tub, which became the focal point of his education. Consequently, he developed as if he were Rousseau's Emile. "In harmony with himself, with everything around him, he develops within nature—if this expression, the only suitable one here, be permitted—like a shrub that extends its vigorous fibers in a fecund, workable soil."[11]

Kornmann's nonmesmerist wife, however, had fallen prey to the aristocratic morality of the "gens en place" (men in power), who had seduced her and destroyed her ties with her family. It was through the intimate mesmeric "rapports" within the family that Bergasse hoped to regenerate France, and so Kornmann's adultery suit against his wife from 1787 to 1789 furnished Bergasse with material for moralistic declamations that, in effect, put the Ancien Régime on trial. In a series of radical pamphlets disguised as legal "mémoires," Bergasse construed Mme. Kornmann's degradation into a parable of the corruptness of French government. He pictured her being tucked into her love nests by the head of the Parisian police (the same Jean-Pierre Lenoir who had alerted the government to the dangers of mesmerism) while the evil spirits of Versailles lurked lecherously in the background, and he elaborated this picture in hundreds of sensational details, which brought out his main theme: the depraved "gens en place" were using their positions to obliterate the "rapports" of French families. It was the conclusion that Bergasse had reached in his mesmerist writings, but now he gave it life by adopting

11. Bergasse, *Considérations*, pp. 63–65, 127; Mesmer's letter, written by Bergasse, in *Journal de Paris*, January 16, 1785, pp. 66–67; *Détail des cures opérées à Buzancy, près Soissons, par le magnétisme animal* (Soissons, 1784), p. 42.

a sentimental style. His *mémoires* read like romantic novels. Kornmann, their hero, suffered as an archetypal martyr of despotism, and his example stood as a warning that any honest bourgeois might share his fate. Bergasse's *mémoires* provided perhaps the most effective barrage of radical propaganda during the prerevolution. They were actually rented and passed around, page by page, in the cafés of the Palais Royal, and Bergasse aimed the last and most explosive of them directly at the ministers, who, in the summer of 1788, were attempting to crush the parlements and to prevent the calling of the Estates General. He demanded the dismissal of the Brienne ministry in an open letter to the king, which appeared on August 8, 1788, and then he fled the country. After the ministry's fall, he returned as a national hero and went on to become a leading member of the Estates General.[12]

In the mid 1780's—before such direct political agitation appeared to be remotely possible—Bergasse concentrated on a more theoretical issue: how would the mesmerized natural man, the young Kornmann, for example, behave in the depraved society of France? Would he not seek "the primitive independence in which Nature made us to be born?" Doctors sensed this danger, Bergasse explained, and therefore they championed their lethal practices as "a means of enervating the human race, of reducing it to the point of having only enough strength to bear docilely the yoke of social institutions." In persecuting mesmerism, doctors served not only their

12. For a detailed account of the Kornmann Affair, see Robert Darnton, "Trends in Radical Propaganda on the Eve of the French Revolution (1782–1788)" (D. Phil. diss., Oxford University, 1964). The most important of Bergasse's legal "mémoires" or "factums" were: *Mémoire pour le sieur Bergasse dans la cause du sieur Kornmann . . .* (1788); *Observations du sieur Bergasse sur l'écrit du sieur de Beaumarchais . . .* (1788); and *Mémoire sur une question d'adultère . . .* (1787).

own interests but also those of the men at the top of the institutions that would collapse in a regenerated, mesmerized France. Bergasse considered medicine "an institution that belongs just as much to politics as to nature," and threatened, writing in the person of an anti-mesmerist doctor: "If by chance animal magnetism really existed . . . I ask you, sir, what revolution should we not of necessity expect? When our generation, exhausted by ills of all kinds and by the remedies supposed to deliver it from those ills, gives way to a vigorous, hardy generation, which knows no other laws of self-preservation than those of Nature: what will become of our habits, our arts, our customs? . . . A more robust constitution would make us remember independence. When, with such a constitution, we necessarily would develop new morals, how could we possibly put up with the yoke of the institutions that govern us today?"[13]

By injecting a Rousseauist bias into a mesmerist analysis of the physical and psychological relations among men, Bergasse saw a way to revolutionize France. He would reverse the historical trend of physico-moral causality, reforming institutions by physically regenerating Frenchmen. Improved bodies would improve morals, and better morals would eventually produce political effects. To be sure, this revolution lacked blood and thunder; it seemed to be a formula of indirect action, involving years of sitting at mesmeric tubs, and it would hardly satisfy the revolutionaries of 1787–1789, when the political crisis had seized the public's attention. Mesmerism was a great attention-seizer earlier in the decade, however, and Bergasse used it to crystallize radical ideas and to communicate a vulgar kind of Rousseauism to a reading public that had not yet awakened to political issues. His political version of Mesmer's

13. All quotations from Bergasse, *Lettre d'un médecin,* pp. 57–66.

innocent quackery had enough bite in it to alarm the Parisian police, and it prepared him for a more influential role as a radical propagandist in 1787 and 1788. Even if it be considered merely the fossilized remains of a dead ideology, mesmerism deserves to be rescued from its forgotten corner in history; for it suggests how abstract political ideas came to life for the French of the 1780's, how the most unlikely issues could be turned into an indictment of the Ancien Régime, and how completely that regime had lost the allegiance of some of the decade's most influential men. In fact mesmerism had taken such a grip on France that its place in history cannot be limited to the 1780's; it continued to mold popular attitudes and interests well into the nineteenth century.

5. FROM MESMER TO HUGO

The mesmerist movement did not die with the Ancien Régime, but the Revolution splintered it and left it to be assimilated in the systems of nineteenth-century philosophers. The nineteenth century possessed few pure mesmerists of the 1780 variety. It produced eclectic thinkers, who attempted to reconstruct general theories from the debris of the Enlightenment. They avoided relying excessively on reason, the old edifice's unifying principle, which had collapsed under the strain of the Revolution. But they also often felt unable to seize on their grandfathers' faith in order to come to grips with the failure of their fathers' rationalism, because the Enlightenment had dealt some damaging blows to religious orthodoxy. Many latter-day philosophes therefore attempted to develop a nonorthodox system that would account for irrationality and for the existence of evil, a consideration that had threatened to upset the balance of Enlightenment thought even before the Terror put an end to the eighteenth century. Religious mysticism provided these philosophers with the richest source of the irrational, for it had flowed through the age of reason, from the convulsionaries to the mesmerists, like an underground stream. When it broke through to the surface after 1789, it had been swollen by Swedenborgianism, martinism, Rosicrucianism, alchemy, physiognomy, and many other currents of spiritualism; but the mesmerist current was one of the most powerful. To chart the main twists and turns of its course from 1789 to about 1850 will serve to put the mesmerism of the 1780's into perspective and to make clear its role in the transition from the Enlightenment to romanticism. The clusters of attitudes generally attached to these two labels might be understood better by tracing a line of thought from one extreme—the eighteenth-century's faith in the ability of reason to decode the laws of nature—to another—the nineteenth century's fascination with the supernatural and the irrational.

Postrevolutionary mesmerists developed their own version of the ideas that characterized spiritualism in general. They emphasized the interaction of physical and moral laws of nature and typically championed "Newtonian" theories of ethics and politics; they produced pseudoscientific analyses of light, electricity, and other forces; they believed in a primitive natural society, known by fragments of a primitive language, and they held a corresponding belief in a primitive religion that included elements of pantheism, theocracy, sabaism, astrology, millenarianism, metempsychosis, and the conviction that a hierarchy of spirits linked man and God. To these ideas—the stock in trade of many spiritualists—the mesmerists added their peculiar supply of medical theories, their fluid, and their practice of somnambulism, which they usually explained as a state in which the inner sense made contact with the spiritual world, freeing the inner man to wander through space and time while his body remained fixed in a trance. Mesmerist followers of Lavater spread the belief that the mind's faculties, especially the will, could be read in one's face and could bring others under one's influence by projecting fluid from the eyes; and other mesmerists grafted many more foreign doctrines onto the theories of Mesmer and Bergasse, for they welcomed any idea that promised to help them in their main endeavor, to climb from the material to the spiritual world. They began, of course, from the most elevated point of prerevolutionary mesmerism, where somnambulism had associated the movement with martinism, Swedenborgianism, and other forms of spiritualism.

Bergasse himself concentrated on earthly affairs for the first nine months of 1789. He helped lead the faction that favored making France into a conservative constitutional monarchy. As the Revolution moved leftward, however, he retreated into the realm of the spirit, accompanied by the Duchesse de Bourbon, the only member of her family—with the notable exception of her brother, Philippe Egalité, the former Duc d'Orléans—to accept the Revolution. The duchess also shared the visions of two of the most extraordinary mystics turned up by the Revolution—Suzette Labrousse and Cathérine Théot. The Revolution provided Mlle. Labrousse with material for apocalyptic prophecies and declamations against the nobility and clergy. The duchess published these in a *Journal prophétique* edited by Pierre Pontard, an intriguer who helped launch Suzette on a public career and made sure that her prophecies followed the Jacobin line. Suzette represented the most extreme political version of mesmerism, but she did not neglect its medical mission. She performed several mesmerist cures and abandoned her treatments only in obedience to her visions, which commanded her to make a pilgrimage by foot to Rome. There she intended to convert the pope and was jailed as a lunatic. Cathérine Théot, "the Mother of God," had been confined for the same reason before the Revolution. Upon her release in 1789, when she was 83, she announced that she would inaugurate the apocalypse by giving birth to God. She presided at mystic services in the home of a widow Godefroy, and she, too, became the pawn of political intriguers. Some agents of the Committee of General Security apparently tried to bring down Robespierre in the spring of 1794 by having her dictate a letter of congratulations to him for honoring her son in the cult of the Supreme Being and for carrying out his mission, which had been foretold by the prophet Ezekiel. Robespierre snuffed out the plot, whose purpose apparently was to discredit him by showing his supposed messianic pretensions, but the incident helped to isolate him from his colleagues on the Committee of Public Safety and thus to prepare his downfall. It is difficult to say how much mesmerism entered into the séances of Cathérine Théot; there must have been some elements of it, for the mystic mesmerist companions of the Duchesse de Bourbon were implicated in the affair. The duchess apparently became a follower of Cathérine under the influence of Dom Gerle, a former prior who took up the Mother of God's cause after abandoning Suzette Labrousse to Pierre Pontard. Magdalene Schweizer, a devout mesmerist and friend of the duchess and of Bergasse, later wrote that she had become an ardent supporter of Cathérine; and Bergasse was arrested and very nearly guillotined because of his connections with the duchess' circle of mystics.[1]

The Revolution brought a reversal in Brissot's mesmerist convictions as abrupt as the change that it made in his fortune—in fact, the two may have been connected. Perhaps Brissot turned against mesmerism because he had no more use for it once he had acquired the power and prestige that had been denied him before the Revolution. This denial had inspired his conversion to mesmerism in 1785. By 1790 he had moved to the center of affairs; and, as editor of the *Patriote français,* he kept an eye on suspicious movements beyond the circumference of the new revolutionary orthodoxy. Thus, in mid-1790, after joining the Comité de Recherches of the municipality of Paris, he announced the danger of a "contre-révolution de somnambules." Two men had attempted to communicate a reactionary program to the king by means of mesmeric fluid, he reported. They had received the message from Madame Thomassin, a som-

1. Much of this and the following account is indebted to Auguste Viatte's fundamental work, *Les Sources occultes du romantisme: illuminisme—théosophie, 1770–1820,* 2 vols. (Paris, 1928). On the circle of the Duchesse de Bourbon, see *Lavaters Beziehungen zu Paris in den Revolutionsjahren 1789–1795,* ed. G. Finsler (Zurich, 1898), esp. pp. 23–25, and Magdalene Schweizer's letters to J. C. Lavater of December 23, 1789, and August 19, 1790, pp. 27*–30*. A good summary of the Théot Affair is in J. M. Thompson, *Robespierre* (Oxford, 1935), II, 210–212. The details of Bergasse's arrest are in his folders in the Archives Nationales, W 479 and F7 4595. The latter includes his pamphlet, *Réflexions du citoyen Bergasse sur sa translation à Paris,* in which he said that he had met Dom Gerle only once and had not seen the Duchesse de Bourbon in four years.

nambulist with aristocratic connections, who had received it herself from the Virgin Mary; and they had attempted to "imprint" it mesmerically on the king's mind at Saint Cloud, where they were arrested—much to their surprise, as they had believed themselves invisible. In another séance, Madame Thomassin had dictated a memoir on a counterrevolutionary plot involving the navies of England and Spain, the Duc d'Orléans, Mirabeau, the Duc de Liancourt, and Alexandre and Charles Lameth. Their confederation, as predicted by Nostradamus, would inaugurate the apocalypse, since "the political revolution of France is purely the initiation of a religious, moral and political revolution, universal throughout the earth." Brissot found these "dangerous ideas, which tend toward a counterrevolution" serious enough to warrant attack. His own experience with somnambulism may have made him genuinely afraid of a Feuillant millennium, but the tone of his attacks suggested political rather than mystical fear. He ridiculed mesmerist illuminism just as its opponents had done, much to his indignation, before the Revolution. Now Brissot wrote like an inverted Barruel: "The sects of illuminists are increasing instead of diminishing; is this not perhaps a result of France's political circumstances, which rally to their mysterious doctrine the men who are unhappy with the new order of things and who hope to find in it the means for destroying [this new order]?"[2]

A mad Welshman named James Tilly Matthews gave a final twist to the political messages transmitted by

2. J.-P. Brissot, *Rapport sur l'affaire de MM. Dhosier et Petit-Jean*, reprinted in *La Révolution française* (1882), II, 593–618; all quotations from pp. 600, 613, 594. For the details of this affair and the polemics it aroused, see also Stanislas de Clermont-Tonnerre, *Nouvelles observations sur les comités des recherches* (Paris, 1790); Brissot, *J. P. Brissot, membre du comité de recherches de la municipalité à Stanislas Clermont . . .* (Paris, 1790); Brissot, *Réplique de J. P. Brissot à Stanislas Clermont . . .* (Paris, 1790); and the articles by Brissot in his *Patriote françois* of July 3 and 5 and August 2 and 6, 1790.

Mesmer's fluid during the Revolution. Matthews received proposals for an Anglo-French peace sent fluidically to him in Paris by the British government in 1794. For a while his project received serious consideration by the Committee of Public Safety; but the Committee finally decided to jail him—on the grounds of suspected Dantonism, however, not false credentials.[3]

Mesmerism exerted a more pervasive though less obvious influence on the Revolution through the Cercle Social, an association of mystic revolutionaries who hoped to establish a Universal Confederation of Friends of the Truth with a masonic organization. The ideology of the Cercle Social derived from a strain of occultism expressed most fully by Restif de la Bretonne, the novelist famous as the "Rousseau du ruisseau" (Rousseau of the gutter). Restif's baroque imagination produced a cosmology made up of animal planets that produced life by copulation; pythagorean spirits that evolved with each incarnation through a hierarchy of stones, plants, animals, and creatures inhabiting countless worlds of countless solar systems; and a pantheistic god who endlessly created universes by a process of crystallization and then destroyed them by absorption in the sun, the brain of the universal "Great Animal." Restif lubricated this animalistic, sexual cosmos with "intellectual fluid" that, like Mesmer's fluid, acted as the intermediary between God and man's internal sense. "God is the material and intellectual brain of the single great animal, of the All, whose intelligence is an actual fluid, like light, but much less dense, as it does not touch any of our external senses and acts only upon the inner sense." Restif claimed to have received his theories from Nature, not from Mesmer or anyone else, except perhaps Mirabeau, whose similar

3. David Williams, "Un document inédit sur la Gironde," *Annales historiques de la Révolution française*, XV (1938), 430–431.

treatise on "high physics," now apparently lost, Restif summarized in *La Philosophie de Monsieur Nicolas.*[4]

Whatever their source, Restif's ideas and others akin to mesmerism emerged in *La Bouche de fer,* the organ of the Cercle Social, which was produced by Restif's friend, Nicolas de Bonneville. Here subscribers could read about the animal planets, the transmigration of souls, the primitive religion and language, and, also, universal harmony. They were informed that the Cercle Social intended "to propagate at last the principles of that divine harmony that must make Nature and Society agree." Bonneville constantly insisted on the interaction of physical and moral law; and he intended his scientific metaphors to be taken literally. Thus he italicized his description of nature's fundamental principles: "Their hidden, fundamental moving force will teach you that the *pure* and *free word,* the burning image of truth, will be able to enlighten everything by its active heat, to *magnetize* everything by its *gravitational* power, to *electrify* excellent *conductors,* to *organize* men, nations and the universe." Bonneville scrambled such occult politico-scientific ideas, in poetry and prose, throughout his works. He drew heavily on the pseudoscientific trends of the 1780's and owed much to mesmerism. Although he rarely referred to Mesmer, he used the Cercle Social to promote Carra's works, which had much in common with his own, and he was identified with the martinists and somnambulists by La Harpe. Bonneville even indicated a mesmerist conviction that mirrors and music reinforced the fluid's action on the internal sense. He referred to man as an *"animated* mirror of nature" (miroir *animé* de la nature)

---

4. Restif de la Bretonne, *Monsieur Nicolas ou le coeur humain dévoilé* (Paris, 1959), vols. V and VI, which contain *La Philosophie de Monsieur Nicolas;* quotations from V, 278–279. Restif was a close friend of L.-S. Mercier, who became an advocate of mesmerism and a collaborator of Carra's.

and described the state of mystic illumination in terms that could have been used by Bergasse: "What is that divine harp, in the hands of nature's God, whose universal cords, attached to all hearts, ceaselessly bind and rebind them? It is truth. All nations hark to the feeblest sounds that leave it, everything senses the divine influence of the universal harmony."[5]

The political ideas of Bonneville and the Abbé Claude Fauchet, who founded the Cercle Social with him, derived from well-known authors like Rousseau and Mably, but they also showed kinship with Carra's and Court de Gébelin's ideal of primitive, natural society. Bonneville and Fauchet preached the communism of primitive Christians and primitives in general (whom they took to be naturally sociable, just as Bergasse had done in criticizing Rousseau). They demanded the redistribution of property by means of an agrarian law and strict limits on inheritances. Restif himself published a communist manifesto in *La Philosophie de Monsieur Nicolas* and possibly wrote articles for the Cercle Social, but he seems rarely to have gone beyond the role of a timid and occasionally outraged observer of the Revolution. Bonneville and Fauchet, however, pursued an extreme, pro-Cordelier and anti-Jacobin line; and during the first sessions of the Cercle Social in October 1790 they preached their mystic political doctrines to audiences of several thousand, including Brissot, Paine, Condorcet, Siéyès, Desmoulins, Mme. Roland, and other revolutionary leaders. The Cercle Social broke up during the crisis of the summer of 1791, and its leaders aligned themselves solidly with the Girondists during the next few months. Bonneville collaborated with Brissot, Clavière, and Condorcet in the *Chronique du mois,* a Girondist paper, and Fauchet went

5. *La Bouche de fer,* October 1790, p. 21; Nicolas de Bonneville, *De l'esprit des religions* (Paris, 1791), pp. 189–190, 75, 152: For the reference to Carra, see *Cercle Social* (Paris, 1790), pp. 353–360; and for La Harpe's remark, see *Mercure de France,* December 25, 1790, p. 119.

to the guillotine with the nineteen other Girondist leaders on October 31, 1793.[6]

The communist ideas of Fauchet and Bonneville might have led them to the extreme left of the Revolution, but their penchant for communication with spirits, fraternal organizations, and grand oratory aligned them with Roland and Brissot. They believed in utopian communism, a communism of universal harmony. Although they might have accepted Marat's theories of fire and light, they could not follow him into the streets and into the sewers, and their attitudes typified those of the other Girondists. Charles Nodier's version of the Girondist Last Supper in the Conciergerie stresses Carra's influence, by means of the German mesmerist-illuminist Dr. André Seiffert, on the philosophy of Bonneville and of Nodier himself, who also dabbled in mesmerism, and it gives a vivid picture of Carra talking cosmology to Brissot before facing the guillotine. It is a fictional version, but its emphasis on the Girondists' theatrical speeches and romantic visions captures the spirit of the Revolution at its most illuministic if not enlightened stage.[7]

The mesmerist episodes of the Revolution represented only occasional flare-ups of a movement dissipated by emigration and social upheaval. During the Napoleonic and Restoration periods the mesmerists came together again, and the movement swelled and gained

6. Restif produced pamphlets attacking the Abbé Maury for Mirabeau, according to Frantz Funck-Brentano, *Restif de la Bretonne: portraits et documents inédits* (Paris, 1928), p. 372. These pamphlets show kinship with the articles in *Cercle Social*, pp. 175–176 and 182–184. See also Jules Charrier, *Claude Fauchet, évêque constitutionnel du Calvados, député à l'Assemblée Législative et à la Convention (1744–1795)* (Paris, 1909), and Philippe Le Harivel, *Nicolas de Bonneville, pré-romantique et révolutionnaire, 1760–1828* (Strasbourg, 1923).

7. Charles Nodier, *Le Dernier banquet des Girondins*, in *Souvenirs de la Révolution et de l'Empire* (Paris, 1850), I, 179–285.

momentum until once more it expressed the outlook of many literate Frenchmen. But the Revolution had changed its course, as can be seen in the spiritualist doctrine of P. S. Dupont de Nemours. There hardly seems a less likely candidate for conversion to spiritualism than Dupont, the clear-headed, physiocratic friend of Turgot and Lavoisier. Indeed, he included a metaphor about a watchmaker God and a remarkably accurate summary of Lavoisier's chemical theory in his spiritualist *Philosophie de l'univers;* but on the very page of his explanation of oxygen, Dupont suggested that the world was a huge animal and men but insects upon it. He continued, in the style of a Turgot, to develop the ideas of a Restif or a Carra: a chain of invisible spirits stretches between us and God; the spirits communicate with our sixth sense by means of an invisible fluid; our souls migrate through the mineral, vegetable, and animal worlds (judging from his physiognomy, Dupont thought he might have been a dog in his last incarnation), and travel among the stars until at last they find peace as "Optimates" at the highest stage of being. Dupont did not admit to mesmerist beliefs, but he had much in common with the mesmerists. He identified health with virtue and said that sickness ended by a "crisis"; and if he used the latest scientific term, caloric, to describe his interplanetary fluid, he made it resemble the vitalistic principle of fire that Carra and other mesmerists adopted from the theories of the grandfather of phlogistonists, G. E. Stahl. Dupont propounded a scientific theory of the interaction of physical and moral forces; he addressed his treatise to Lavoisier and wrote it while hiding from the Terror in an observatory under the protection of the astronomer J. J. Lalande.

The point is not that Dupont was a crypto-mesmerist, but that he was hiding, that he expected to be ripped from the observatory and guillotined at any moment, and that he wrote the *Philosophie de l'univers* as a final credo, a testament for his friends and children. He thought that it must incorporate the scientific advances of the century and that it must not repudiate Voltaire's victories over superstition; yet it must have room for something more than the cold science and rationalism of the Ancien Régime. It must account for the bloodshed and the Terror that keep interrupting its narrative with the suggestion that God must be either evil or impotent. The Terror had penetrated the sanctuary of science in which Dupont was hiding and had brought him face to face with the greatest problem of the eighteenth-century philosophers, the need of a theodicy. Condorcet, in exactly the same position, answered this need by positing the existence of "Progress," a force that would triumph over "superstition" in some future age. Dupont also invoked two forces, "Oromasis," the good spirit, and "Arimane," the inferior spirit of death; but he acknowledged that he was writing a poem, that the spirits and subspirits were invisible genies that might, perhaps, snatch one from under the guillotine's blade, and might not. The old belief in the forward march of Reason could not sustain him; he drew back into spiritualism, and so felt able to defy Robespierre and Danton. "Such is, my friends, the doctrine that I wanted to expose to you before dying . . . Such is *my Religion* . . . and I now shall permit the tyrants to send my *monad* forth to prostrate itself before the ETERNEL. Valete et me amate. 10 June 1793."[8]

Dupont survived the Revolution, but his retreat into spiritualism signaled the death of the Enlightenment. After the Terror, mesmerists might be revolutionaries

8. P. S. Dupont de Nemours, *Philosophie de l'univers* (Paris), quotation from p. 236. "Monad" was Dupont's expression for the soul. It suggested the Leibnizian concern for the inner, vitalistic principles of matter as opposed to Newtonian mathematical analysis. On these two basic trends in eighteenth-century science, see the first two chapters of Ernest Cassirer's *The Philosophy of the Enlightenment*, tr. F. C. A. Koelln and J. P. Pettegrove (Princeton, 1955).

like Bonneville or conservatives like the older Bergasse, but they would not build their temples on the foundation of Reason. The ideas of Fabre d'Olivet show the direction that the conservative mesmerists took and also their predilection for temple-building. He attempted to construct a new religion with the usual materials of spiritualism—metempsychosis, primitive language, communications with a hierarchy of spirits—and with mesmerism. His numerous mesmerist cures persuaded him that the fluid acted as the medium between man's will and nature, which he conceived as the will of the "universal man" composed of all individuals. "Mesmeric fluid is none other than the universal man himself, affected and put in movement by one of his emanations." It was by the fluid's action on the will, not by reason, that Fabre cured the sick, communicated with ghosts, and, in the highest somnambulist state, acquired knowledge of God, science, and political theory. The hierarchy of spirits provided Fabre with a model for the organization of men on earth: he would keep citizens stratified in classes by reinforcing tradition and authority. Hostile to the revolutionary ideal of equality, he favored monarchical government—or, better yet, a theocracy to be created by Napoleon, perhaps with Fabre himself as pontiff. It was an appropriate philosophy for the Empire, for Joséphine de Beauharnais consulted some of the mesmerist fortune-tellers who survived the Revolution, and so did Napoleon, if the memoirs of the Comte d'Allonville, a mesmerist friend of Bergasse and d'Eprémesnil, are to be believed. "What is more bizarre still, General Bonaparte, when about to leave for his first campaign in Italy, wanted to have the fate that awaited him in the army predicted by the somnambulist Mally-Châteaurenaud [possibly the same Châteaurenaud who had been a member of the Society of Harmony] . . . Bonaparte believed that the Battle of Castiglione fulfilled the prediction of the somnambulist, whom he again carefully had sought out before his departure for Egypt."[9]

Fabre's mystic, theocratic conservatism had much in common with that of Joseph de Maistre, who spent some of his long evenings in St. Petersburg assimilating the ideas of Saint-Martin, Swedenborg, Willermoz, and evidently several other mesmerists. De Maistre found the theory of mesmerism already formulated in the writings of Swedenborg; in fact he traced it all the way back to Solon, but his researches apparently failed to convert him to the mesmerist movement. Mesmerism exerted more influence on another political system that came out of Russia and that eventually was taken to be conservative—the Holy Alliance. The Alliance's idealized brotherhood of Christians under the sovereignty of God, "la parole de vie" (the word of life), had been inspired in part by the Baronne de Krüdener, a mystic of the mesmerist-martinist-physiognomist variety who had won the confidence of Tsar Alexander I by revealing the religious character of his mission to destroy Napoleon, the Antichrist. When Mme. de Krüdener arrived in Paris with the Russian troops in 1815, she gathered around her the patriarchs of mesmerism, Bergasse and Puységur, and its matriarch, the Duchesse de Bourbon. Bergasse had been reduced by then to an ill-furnished gardener's cottage

9. *Mémoires secrets de 1770 à 1820 par M. le Comte d'Allonville, auteur des Mémoires tirés des papiers d'un homme d'état* (Paris, 1838–1845), VI, 12–13. Fabre's statement is quoted in Léon Cellier, *Fabre d'Olivet: contribution à l'étude des aspects religieux du romantisme* (Paris, 1953), p. 321, which mentions Joséphine's mesmerist connections (p. 181) and which is the source for the above account of Fabre's ideas. Napoleon later considered Mesmer, Lavater, and Gall to be quacks, according to the *Journal of the Private Life and Conversations of the Emperor Napoleon at Saint Helena by the Count de Las Cases* (London, 1825), III, 66–68. Of course, no memoirs about Napoleon can be trusted. Even the *Journal du magnétisme* (Paris, 1847), pp. 239–253, a storehouse of Napoleonic legends, wisely refused to make him into a mesmerist.

in the outskirts of Paris, but the tsar did not hesitate to visit him, accompanied by Mme de Krüdener, and to consult him several times on the millenium of universal harmony to be established in Europe. According to one source, Bergasse wrote a draft of the Holy Alliance. He certainly influenced it and tried to maintain his influence in later years by corresponding with the tsar.[10]

Mme. de Krüdener's arrival in Paris coincided with the revival of mesmerism and other spiritualist vogues, a revival that continued intermittently through the July Monarchy and the Second Empire. Her own séances attracted the most fashionable Parisians of the first years of the Restoration, but her following declined as the apocalypse she predicted refused to arrive on schedule and as her prophecies, after her separation from Alexander, increasingly echoed the liberal views of her friend Benjamin Constant. The beau monde found a more attractive prophet in the beautiful Indian somnambulist Alina d'Elder; it flocked to the mesmerist sessions of Dr. Koreff, Mlle. Lenormand, and the Abbé Faria (who made water taste like champagne) and later patronized the mystic, masonic mesmerism of Henri Delaage. The working classes turned, in times of need, to the more obscure mesmerist fortune-tellers that Balzac found everywhere in the seedy sections of Paris during the July Monarchy. By the time of mesmerism's apogee in the 1850's, new techniques had evolved for summoning ghosts and triggering convulsions. The mesmerized wands and chains remained but the tubs were generally abandoned; mirrors had been perfected so that they

10. On de Maistre and Mesmer, see Emile Dermenghem, *Joseph de Maistre mystique* (Paris, 1946), p. 47; on Bergasse's relations with Alexander and Mme. de Krüdener, see Louis Bergasse, *Un défenseur des principes traditionnels sous la Révolution, Nicolas Bergasse* (Paris, 1910), pp. 257–263. The literature on Mme. de Krüdener, which has tended to minimize her influence on the Holy Alliance, is summarized in E. J. Knapton, "An unpublished letter of Mme. de Krüdener," *Journal of Modern History*, IX (1937), 483–492.

showed spirits instead of merely reinforcing the movement of the fluid; spirits communicated their messages
by means of rapping tables and charcoal drawings; and
the old-fashioned mesmerist massagers had surrendered
the command of the movement to the somnambulists.
A modern mesmerist, like Alphonse Cahagnet, spent all
his time communicating with ghosts, who telegraphed
snatches of poetry, their regards to their families, and
descriptions of heaven to a medium or, very often, to
a table, which rapped out their messages in a sort of
morse code.

While these innovations developed, the apostolic
succession continued from Bergasse and Puységur to
J. P. F. Deleuze and then to the Baron Du Potet. The
Society of Universal Harmony, which had collapsed with
most of its provincial affiliates in 1789, was restored in
1815 under Puységur as the Society of Mesmerism (Societé
du Magnétisme) and was reorganized in 1842. By the
1850's, when Du Potet had taken command of the movement, the faithful met twice a week in rooms over the
restaurant of the Frères Provençaux of the Palais Royal.
The sessions did not recreate the splendor of the old
meetings at the Hôtel de Coigny, but they were well
attended and cheaper (admission, 15 sous); and the new
organization, in keeping with the more commercial
spirit of the time, kept regular office hours, saved its
funds diligently, and published a monthly *Journal du
magnétisme* (20 volumes, 1845–1861). Mesmerism's revival aroused its natural enemies, the orthodox doctors
and scientists, who fought it once more with the tried
and true weapons of ridicule and academic commissions.
The Théâtre des Variétés produced a successful satire on
mesmerism, *La Magnétisomanie,* in 1816, and in 1825
the Academy of Medicine began a series of investigations
and debates that set off a new wave of pamphleteering.
In 1831 the academicians appeared to end their fifty-
year war against the mesmerists by hearing a report

from an investigative commission that conceded some therapeutic value to mesmerism. But the academy returned to the attack in 1837; following a hostile report from yet another commission, it cleverly offered a prize of 5,000 francs to any mesmerist who could read without using his eyes. In 1840, after all competitors had failed, it finally refused to deal with mesmerism any more, relegating it to the limbo of useless issues like the squaring of the circle. Mesmerism fared better elsewhere, however. By midcentury the relatively modest varieties of fluidism and somnambulism were being studied seriously throughout Europe. Shortly before his death in 1815, Mesmer himself had given his blessing to the establishment of a mesmerist course in the University of Berlin. James Braid had begun the investigation of induced hypnosis in England, and French hypnotists, led by J. M. Charcot, were to exert an important influence on the development of Freudian psychology.[11]

Mesmerism also continued to inspire political theorists—not merely the mystic conservatives who pursued the lines of thought developed by Fabre d'Olivet, but also liberals and utopian socialists, who carried on the Restif-Bonneville tradition. Pierre Ballanche, the leading postrevolutionary mystic of Lyons, flirted with most illuminist doctrines, including mesmerism, and aligned himself with the conservative, theocratic ideas of Fabre and

11. One of the most interesting contemporary accounts of nineteenth-century mesmerism is Alexandre Erdan, *La France mistique* [sic]: *tableau des excentricités religieuses de ce tems* [sic] (Paris, 1855), I, 40–177. The *Journal du Magnétisme* is an excellent but unwieldy source, and Charles Burdin and E. F. Dubois, *Histoire académique du magnétisme animal* . . . (Paris, 1841), contains a detailed but biased survey of the battles between mesmerists and academicians. Balzac's report on mesmerism is in chapter 13 of *Le Cousin Pons*. The connections between mesmerism, Christian Science, and Freudian psychology are traced in Stefan Zweig, *Mental Healers: Franz Anton Mesmer, Mary Baker Eddy, Sigmund Freud,* tr. Eden and Cedar Paul (New York, 1932), and in Frank Podmore, *From Mesmer to Christian Science: A Short History of Mental Healing* (New York, 1963).

Joseph de Maistre; but he also gave a start to the most important mystic opponent of capitalism, Charles Fourier. It was in Ballanche's *Bulletin de Lyon* that Fourier announced his discovery of Universal Harmony, the guiding principle of his philosophy. For Fourier, as for Bergasse, Universal Harmony was to rule in the future utopian state that would follow the imminent apocalypse. "It is necessary to throw all political, moral and economic theories into the fire and to prepare for the most astonishing event . . . FOR THE SUDDEN TRANSITION FROM SOCIAL CHAOS TO UNIVERSAL HARMONY." Like Bergasse, Fourier built his system on the analogy between physical and moral laws of nature. He, too, claimed to be the Newton of politics: "I soon recognized that the laws of passionate Gravity conformed in all respects to those of material Gravity, which Newton and Leibniz had explained, and that there was a COMMON SYSTEM OF MOVEMENT FOR THE MATERIAL AND FOR THE SPIRITUAL WORLD." In spite of its many similarities with Fourier's *Théorie des quatre mouvements*, Bergasse's *Considérations sur le magnétisme animal* would have been one of the books on Fourier's bonfire; for Fourier imagined burning all books but his own. He denied indebtedness to any author. He alone had discovered the natural law of society, the gravitational pull of passion, and this must be put to work, instead of being repressed, in order to organize men in a universal brotherhood. But Fourier's claims to originality hid only the exact point at which he came into his mesmerist inheritance; the mesmerist influence is evident in many of his works, even in details like his defense of water witching, his fluidic theory of light and heat, and his stress on the three principles of the mesmerist trinity—God, matter, and movement. Fourier's preference for primitive, natural society as opposed to "civilization" recalled Bergasse and Court de Gébelin as well as Rousseau, and his pride in his humble position as "sergeant of a shop" (sergent de boutique) echoed the mesmerists' denunciations of academicians. "But if the discovery is the work of an unknown, a provincial type or a scientific pariah, of one of those intruders who, like Prion, have the fault of not even being academicians, he is bound to draw down upon his head all the anathemas of the cabal." Fourier even condemned the faculty of medicine for persecuting mesmerism, which he finally incorporated into his own system by explaining that the mesmerists had misused and misunderstood their science. Contact with the other world was really to be explained by the operation of the somnambulist's "ultrahuman faculty"; somnambulism proved the immortality of the soul; and if it had been abused in "civilization," it would be "in great fashion, of great utility, in the state of harmony."[12]

While Fourier assimilated mesmerism as one of many foreign elements (including the transmigration of souls and the copulating planets) in a vision that was ultimately his own, his followers hardly can be distinguished from the radical mesmerists of the midcentury. Just Muiron came to Fourierism by way of mesmerism, and Joseph Olivier and Victor Hennequin fit Mesmer's cosmology into the roomy "infiniverse" (infinivers) of Fourier. Fourier himself had refused to be mesmerized on his deathbed, but he communicated mesmerically with his disciples after his death; and the spirits that talked at

12. Charles Fourier, *Théorie des quatre mouvements et des destinées générales: prospectus et annonce de la découverte,* in *Oeuvres complètes de Ch. Fourier* (Paris, 1841–1848), I, xxxvi, 12, 102, 23; Fourier, *Théorie de l'unité universelle,* in *Oeuvres complètes,* III, 337; Fourier, *Le Nouveau monde industriel et sociétaire,* in *Oeuvres complètes,* VI, 454–457. Fourier denied having any "notion pratique" of mesmerism. He said that he had read a work by Deleuze, which was enough to convince him that the mesmerists did not understand their fluid, and that seven-eighths of mankind could not experience somnambulism (Fourier, "Des cinq passions sensuelles," *La Phalange: Revue de la science sociale* [Paris, 1846], IV, 123–129). I am indebted to Jonathan Beecher, who guided me through the wonderland of Fourierism and is presently preparing a definitive map of it.

a Fourierist "turning-table" session of 1853 showed excellent command of mesmerism according to the account published by Alexandre Erdan.

M. VINAQUIN—Certainly. Ask the table, that is, the spirit that is inside it; it will tell you that I have above my head an enormous pipe of fluid, which rises from my hair up to the stars. It's an aromatic pipe by which the voice of spirits on Saturn reaches my ear . . . THE TABLE (thumping strongly with its foot)—Yes, yes, yes. Aromatic pipe. Conduit. Aromatic pipe. Conduit. Conduit. Conduit. Conduit. Yes.

This mesmero-fourierism made perfect sense to the mesmerists, who welcomed the adherence of Fourier's followers, published long extracts from Fourier's works, and marveled that Fourier, with only a layman's knowledge of mesmerism gained from a reading of Deleuze, should have "divined by intuition most of mesmerism's secrets."[13]

The mesmerists also welcomed some Saint-Simonians into the fold. Saint-Simon, like Fourier, claimed to be the Newton of a new social science, and he drew parallels between the physical laws of the universe and the moral laws of society. He himself kept his fancy earthbound, but his disciples soared into the upper regions of mysticism, where they often crossed paths with the Fourierists. Saint-Simon's closest early associate, the Comte J. S. E. de Redern, posed as a mesmerist professor and wrote a full-blown mesmerist treatise after splitting with him; and a more faithful follower, Pierre Leroux, associated the cause with a mixture of mesmerism, martinism, and

13. Alexandre Erdan, *La France mistique* [sic], I, 75–76. Charles Pellarin, *The Life of Charles Fourier,* tr. F. G. Shaw, 2 ed. (New York, 1848), p. 225, contains an account of Fourier's deathbed scene. The mesmerist pronouncements on Fourierism are in *Journal du magnétisme,* VI (1848), 337–350 and 368–375; quotation comes from p. 375.

carbonarism that would have delighted Bonneville. Robert Owen completed the hierarchy of radical utopian mesmerists. A letter by Anna Blackwell announced to the readers of the *Journal du magnétisme* in 1853 that "Mr. Owen, the famous socialist . . . who had been until now a materialist in the strongest sense of the word, has been completely converted to the belief in the immortality of the soul by the conversations he has had with members of his family, who have been dead for years." In another letter published by the journal, Owen revealed that he also had communicated with Benjamin Franklin and Thomas Jefferson, whose experience of the other world had apparently weakened their antimesmerist convictions, and the spirits had not restricted their messages to religious matters; in seventeen or eighteen séances they had stressed "that the object of the current general manifestations is to reform the population of our planet, to convince all of us of the truth of another life and to make us all sincerely charitable."

This utopian strain of mesmerism went back to Bergasse's concept of "natural society," to Gébelin's primitive world, and to Carra's third stage of history, modeled on the ideal desert-island community. Even Brissot had planned to establish utopian colonies in France, Switzerland, and the United States. How appropriate, then, was the discovery in 1846 that Mesmer himself had been a utopian radical! From 1846 to 1848, the *Journal du magnétisme* printed installments of a manuscript, *Notions élémentaires sur la morale, l'éducation et la législation pour servir à l'instruction publique en France*, which it said Mesmer had written during the Revolution and had sent to the French National Convention. The *Notions* advanced doctrines worthy of the severest Jacobin: sovereignty belonged solely to the people; law was the expression of the general will; taxation should be used to create the greatest possible equality; and festivals of the Supreme Being should promote "social virtues" among the citizens.

These virtues corresponded closely with those advocated by the Society of Universal Harmony; they would reign in the "harmonie universelle" of the ideal society modeled by Mesmer from material that seemed to come straight out of the theories of Bergasse. The only original element in the *Notions* was an analysis of how civic spirit and perhaps even the general will would operate during civic festivals, which were to be elaborate affairs for promulgating laws, judging legal disputes, holding athletic contests, and celebrating the civil religion. Mesmer explained, "Finally, it will be proven by the principles that form the system of influences or of animal magnetism that it is very important for man's physical and moral harmony to gather frequently in large assemblies . . . where all intentions and wills should be directed toward one and the same object, especially toward the order of nature, while singing and praying together; and that it is in these situations that the harmony that has begun to be upset in some individuals can be reestablished and health fortified." The twin principles of "liberté et santé" (liberty and health) would animate the ideal republic that Mesmer outlined to the Convention. Every citizen would serve society progressively as "enfant," "élève," "défenseur de la patrie," "père de famille et citoyen," "fonctionnaire public," "surveillant," and "vétéran" (infant, pupil, defender of the fatherland, family father and citizen, civil servant, overseer, veteran). Mesmer carefully described the social functions, the age limits, and even the costumes that were to characterize each stage. Careful planning and the proper theory of man and the universe promised to make France into a democracy that would last forever, forever dedicated to liberty and equality. It was a noble plan, the journal commented, noting that it came as close to Fourierism as Fourier had come to mesmerism.

In fact, mesmerism had come full circle with the emergence of the new, revolutionary Mesmer in 1846. It had returned to the themes of the 1780's just in time for another blast of revolutionary propaganda in another revolutionary situation. The passions of Bergasse and Brissot seemed to rage again in the diatribes published in the *Journal du magnétisme* against the dual "despots" of the academies and politics: "Our learned men wanted nothing to do with mesmerism, just as other men wanted nothing to do with liberty . . . [but] the links of the despotic chain that science did not want to break have burst into splinters." Still alive after sixty years of combat, the radical strain of mesmerism, the spirit of 1789, expressed itself for the last time in the mesmerist manifesto of 1848. "Rejoice mesmerists! Here is the dawning of a great and beautiful new day . . . O Mesmer! You who loved the republic . . . you foresaw this time, but . . . you were not understood."[14]

The spell that Mesmer had cast upon the French in the 1780's brought men of letters as well as political scientists under his influence during the first half

14. Redern's mesmerism is mentioned in Henri Gouhier, *La Jeunesse d'Auguste Comte et la formation du positivisme* (Paris, 1936), II, 128–132. The letters from Anna Blackwell and Robert Owen, dated April 2 and May 20, 1853, are in the *Journal du magnétisme*, XII (1853), 199 and 297, and have been retranslated from the French. See also Frank Podmore, *Robert Owen: A Biography* (London, 1906), II, 600–614. Mesmer's *Notions* appeared throughout vols. III–VII (1846–1848) of the *Journal du magnétisme;* the quotations are from III (1846), pp. 251, 94, 38–39, and 98, and V (1847), pp. 99 and 97. Mesmer showed no interest in politics before the Revolution, and his *Mémoire de F.-A. Mesmer sur ses découvertes* (Paris, 1799) is more remarkable for its dubious claim that he discovered somnambulism than for any political views. The story that he timed a trip to Paris in 1793 well enough to salute his old enemy Bailly while Bailly was being carted to the guillotine has no basis in fact. Mesmer did dress up some requests for patronage to the Directory in republican language: see his letters reprinted in the *Journal du magnétisme*, I (1845), 48–51, V (1847), 265, and VIII (1849), 653–656. So it seems possible that he became a late convert to republicanism, and there is no reason to doubt the *Journal du magnétisme*'s claims that it was publishing a genuine, unedited manuscript of Mesmer's. In any case, Mesmer made his first public appearance as a revolutionary in 1846–1848.

of the nineteenth century. Mesmer might be considered the first German romantic to cross the Rhine; he certainly opened up the route for two of the most important German agents among French romantics, Madame de Staël and Dr. D.-F. Koreff. The Baron de Staël, a Swedenborgian friend of Lavater and Saint-Martin, mesmerized with the founders of animal magnetism. His influence on his wife may have been as weak as their marriage, but other mesmerists—the Duchesse de Bourbon and Mme. de Krüdener, to name only the most famous—probably affected her formulation of romanticism. Although Mme. de Staël, like Chateaubriand and Benjamin Constant, managed to live with mesmerists without being converted by them, her respect for their ideas seems to have contributed to her favorable treatment of German mysticism in *De l'Allemagne*. Koreff, a German mesmerist doctor, also helped Mme. de Staël turn away from the Enlightenment philosophy of her youth. During a visit to her retreat at Coppet, he evidently mesmerized her ailing mystic mentor, A. G. de Schlegel, charmed her, and won the reward of a eulogy in *De l'Allemagne*. Koreff acted as a sort of mesmerist literary agent. He knew the most important romantic writers of France and Germany and mesmerized many of them. His successful treatment of Prince Hardenberg brought him a chair in physiology at the University of Berlin and a position as councillor of state, organizer of the new University of Bonn, and one of the most powerful men in Prussian politics and academics. After losing his grip on Hardenberg, Koreff retreated to Paris where his wit, his penetrating glances, his impressive German accent, and his leadership of the mesmerist movement made him a lion of the salons of the Restoration and the July Monarchy. Koreff helped produce and direct the great French vogue of the tales of Hoffmann, his friend and fellow mesmerist; he introduced Heine to the literary circles of Paris; he purveyed the fantastic among Nodier,

Hugo, Balzac, Stendhal, Delacroix, and Chateaubriand; he even acted—unsuccessfully—as doctor to Marie Duplessis, the Dame aux Camélias.[15]

Koreff's triumphal march through the Parisian salons provides only a crude measure of mesmerism's influence; for although he met everyone, he did not convert everyone he met. He doctored his good friend Benjamin Constant without winning him to the cause, and those he won did not necessarily express their faith in their works. French romantic writing is full of electric shocks, occult forces, and ghosts, but it is not easy to determine how many of them were animated by mesmerism. Is the following excerpt from a "harmonie" by Lamartine, for example, merely a metaphor?

> L'harmonieux éther, dans ses vagues d'azur,
> Enveloppe les monts d'un fluide plus pur.

That mesmerism helped lift the poet to his intuitive sense of the infinite is suggested by the fact that the mesmerists of the *Journal du magnétisme* treated him as one of their own. Many other writers received similar treatment. Alexandre Dumas, for example, was great material for mesmerist propaganda. He even wrote some himself, based on his own somnambulist experiments, and he included generous doses of mesmerizing in novels like *Joseph Balsamo*, where Balsamo, a sort of mesmerist Faust, projects fluid from mirrors, pianos, wands, and his eyes, and exults, after a somnambulist session crucial to the plot, "Thus is science no vain word like virtue! Mesmer has defeated Brutus." Mesmerism provided Dumas and many other romantic writers with the material

15. See Viatte, *Les Sources occultes du romantisme*, vol. II, chap. III, and Marietta Martin, *Un aventurier intellectuel sous la Restauration et la Monarchie de Juillet: le docteur Koreff (1783–1851)* (Paris, 1925). The Baron de Staël's mesmerizing is mentioned in *Testament politique de M. Mesmer . . .* (Paris, 1785), p. 20.

they wanted, with a system of what Théophile Gautier called "the fantastic, the mysterious, the occult, the inexplicable." The mesmerists of the 1780's believed that this system harmonized with the rationalism of the Enlightenment. But it also expressed a form of pre-romanticism. According to a pamphlet of 1784, a member of the Society of Harmony proclaimed that the reign of "Voltaire, of the Encyclopedists, is collapsing; that one finally gets tired of everything, especially of cold reasoning; that we must have livelier, more delicious delights, some of the sublime, the incomprehensible, the supernatural."[16]

Because of its unfamiliar vocabulary, mesmerism may elude the lay reader's investigation of French literature. He should be on his guard when he finds a writer like Gautier putting characters "en rapport" by touching one another or overcoming an "obstacle" in one another's "atmosphère." When Gautier arbitrarily interjects a harmonica into a story and permits a character to see the

16. Alphonse de Lamartine, "L'Infini dans les cieux," in *Harmonies poétiques et religieuses,* Classiques Garnier ed. (Paris, 1925), p. 76 (the lines can be translated as: "The harmonious ether, in its azure waves,/Envelops the mountains in a pure fluid"); article on Lamartine in *Journal du magnétisme,* VI (1848), 217–224; Alexandre Dumas, *Mémoires d'un médecin: Joseph Balsamo,* Calmann Lévy ed. (Paris, 1888), III, 113; Théophile Gautier, *Jettatura,* in *Romans et contes,* Charpentier ed. (Paris, 1923), p. 188; *L'Antimagnétisme* . . . (London, 1784), pp. 140–141. Dumas published an account of his mesmerizing in Célestin Gragnon, *Du traitement et de la guérison de quelques maladies chroniques au moyen du somnambulisme magnétique* . . . (Bordeaux, 1859), and he explained the mesmerist inspiration of *Joseph Balsamo* in a letter published by the *Journal du magnétisme,* V (1847), 146–154. The journal later objected to the portrayal of Mesmer in the second part of the novel but applauded the mesmerizing in Dumas' *Urbain Grandier* (ibid., VIII [1849], 152–153, and IX [1850], 228 and 233). A complete mesmerist tour of French and also English, American, and German literature might enlarge our understanding of many writers (notably Poe, Hawthorne, Sand, Hoffmann, Kleist, and Novalis, and even philosophers such as Fichte, Schelling, and Schopenhauer) and of popular tastes in reading, represented by now-forgotten best sellers like Frédéric Soulié's *Le Magnétiseur* (Paris, 1834).

"rayons" (rays) of the soul—which is a "petite lueur
tremblotante" (tiny, trembling gleam) subject to the
"attraction" (gravity) of the will—through the heroine's
skin, he may be assumed to be talking mesmerism. The
assumption turns into a conviction as Gautier sets his
characters to mesmerizing one another by projecting
fluid from their eyes and applying a mesmeric wand and
even a tub to provoke somnambulism. He seems to treat
mesmerism as something more than a Hoffmannesque
phantom, an English dandy, or any other literary prop:
he describes Mesmer's fluid as if it were the medium of
passion, the very stuff of life. The life of Alicia in *Jettatura*
flows out of her body, under the magnetic impulse of
Paul's evil eye, just as life escapes from Octave in *Avatar.*
The "science matérialiste" of "civilisation ignorante"
fails to detect their fatal ennui, for it cannot find their
souls; and Gautier, showing a scorn of orthodox medicine
worthy of Bergasse, calls in occult scientists to treat them.
Horned finger gestures and other devices act as lightning
rods against the "fluide malfaisant" (malevolent fluid)
of the evil eye, but they represent only the remnants
of primitive science contained in the superstitions of
the common people and so fail to rescue Alicia. Octave,
however, is saved by a doctor who has discovered the
primitive science itself, which turns out to be a Hindu
variety of mesmerism that would have delighted Court
de Gébelin and perhaps even the Encyclopedist who had
called for a "new Paracelsus" to create a science of the
soul.[17]

In his essay on Balzac, Gautier revealed that his
fictional accounts of mesmerism and related forms of

17. Gautier, *Avatar,* in *Romans et contes,* pp. 52, 37–39; *Jettatura,*
pp. 211, 221, 129, 190. Mesmerism provided Gautier with a scientific
approach to other forms of the fantastic, notably opium visions (see
"La pipe d'opium," in *Romans et contes*). His mesmerist beliefs are
mentioned in the account of his occultism in H. van der Tuin, *L'Evolution psychologique, esthétique et littéraire de Théophile Gautier: étude de
caractérologie "littéraire"* (Paris and Amsterdam, 1933), pp. 203–220.

romantic science were meant to be taken seriously. The essay showed that he and Balzac sealed their friendship with a common faith in mesmerism. They even planned a treasure hunt to be directed by a somnambulist and experimented with somnambulism under the guidance of Mme. Emile de Girardin, their companion in matters of literature and occult science. Mesmerism inspired Gautier's description of Balzac as a "voyant" with a heady sense of realism, a "somnambule" with his feet on the ground, an "avatar" with an enormous, phrenological memory bump and eyes that could read through one's chest by mighty jets of mesmeric fluid. And mesmerism determined the formula for success that Balzac passed on to Gautier: "He [Balzac] wanted to be a great man and he became one by incessant projections of that fluid which is more powerful than electricity and which he analyzed so subtly in *Louis Lambert*."[18]

Gautier was referring to the fragments of Lambert's "Théorie de la Volonté" (Theory of the Will), which explained, with appropriate reference to "Mesmer's discovery, so important and still so badly appreciated," that man could make direct contact with the spiritual world and could also control life on earth by exerting his willpower, that is, by directing fluid from his inner sense or "inner vision" through all obstacles, space, and time. Balzac's Lambert had succeeded Newton. He had discovered the secret realm where the material and the spiritual met, and he passed from the former into the latter, where he remained in a state of Hindu-like "ecstasy," very like the "extase" described in many issues of the *Journal du magnétisme* and the catalepsy in the Barberinist strain of mesmerism. All mesmerists emphasized the importance of the will. For example, Henri Delaage, a typical mesmerist of Balzac's time, expounded

18. Théophile Gautier, "Honoré de Balzac," in *Portraits contemporains: littérateurs—peintres—sculpteurs—artistes dramatiques,* Charpentier ed. (Paris, 1874), pp. 48, 63, 58, 88, 71.

ideas that hardly can be distinguished from those of Balzac and Lambert. "There exists a very subtle magnetic fluid, the link in man between soul and body; without a particular seat, it circulates through all the nerves, which it stretches and loosens at the command of the will; its color is that of the electric spark . . . Glances from the eye, those rays of the spirit of life, are the mysterious chain that links souls sympathetically across space." Delaage remarked, "The will, H. de Balzac told us one day, is the moving force of the imponderable fluid, and the [body's] members are the conducting agents of it." To make the point even clearer, Delaage's exposition of classic mesmerism was published with a long excerpt from *Ursule Mirouet,* where Balzac expatiated on "the doctrine of Mesmer, who recognized in man a penetrating influence . . . put to work by the will, curative by the abundance of the fluid . . ." Balzac did not restrict mesmerism to the theoretical sections of his novels. He built it into his characters, whose passions vibrated along waves of the "vital fluid" that was treated as the essence of life in *Le Centenaire ou les deux Béringheld.* Raphaël recognized that this force was also the essence of love, thanks to his own "Théorie de la Volonté" in *La Peau de chagrin;* and in his foreword to *La Comédie Humaine,* Balzac explained that it occupied a place of great importance in his panorama of life in the early nineteenth century. "Animal magnetism, whose miracles I have familiarized myself with since 1820; the fine research of Gall, Lavater's successor, and, in short, all those who have studied thought the way opticians have studied light, two virtually similar things, confirm the ideas both of the mystics, those disciples of Saint John the Apostle, and of the great thinkers who have established the spiritual world."[19]

19. Honoré de Balzac, *Louis Lambert,* Marcel Bouteron and Jean Pommier ed. (Paris, 1954), p. 95; *Instruction explicative et pratique des tables tournantes . . . par Ferdinand Silas, précédée d'une introduction sur*

This statement indicates that several other philosophers besides Mesmer helped boost Balzac into the supernatural. Balzac found Swedenborg especially helpful and wrote *Séraphîta* as a Swedenborgian formulation of such spiritualist doctrines as metempsychosis, primitive religion, the chain of spirits, and even the animated planets. But *Séraphîta* offers the version of Swedenborgianism that was common among mesmerists. Its first chapter can be read as an account of somnambulism, and its third chapter expresses Balzac's belief that Swedenborg beat Mesmer to the discovery of animal magnetism. Similarly, Balzac's main mesmerist novel, *Ursule Mirouet*, describes a mesmerist character as a "Swedenborgist." The overlapping references are understandable, for Swedenborg and Mesmer provided Balzac with the same message: the attempt of scientists to weigh and measure the exterior of things was blinding them to the greater problem of understanding the inner being. Balzac also might have extracted this message from the works of Diderot and Leibniz or of other writers he admired. He

---

l'action motrice du fluide magnétique par Henri Delaage, troisième édition, augmentée d'un chapitre sur le rôle du fluide magnétique dans le mécanisme de la volonté par H. de Balzac (Paris, 1853), pp. 6–12; Balzac, "Avant-Propos" to *La Comédie Humaine,* in *Oeuvres complètes,* Marcel Bouteron and Henri Longnon ed. (Paris, 1912), p. xxxv. Despite Balzac's avowals of his mesmerist beliefs, little of the extensive literature on him has dealt with them. Well-known works like Albert Prioult, *Balzac avant la Comédie Humaine (1818–1829)* (Paris, 1936), and André Maurois, *Prométhée ou la vie de Balzac* (Paris, 1965), barely mention his mesmerism, although it is treated more fully in Moïse Le Yaouanc, *Nosographie de l'humanité Balzacienne* (Paris, 1959), F. Bonnet-Roy, *Balzac, les médecins, la médecine et la science* (Paris, 1944), and Henri Evans, *Louis Lambert et la philosophie de Balzac* (Paris, 1951). As might be expected, the mesmerists themselves recognized the pervasive role of their doctrine in Balzac's novels. The *Journal du magnétisme* celebrated Balzac as "of all renowned authors . . . the one who has studied mesmerism the most" (IV, 284). Treating his theory of the will as standard mesmerism, it printed his account of the origins of Dr. Bouvard, the mesmerist character in *Ursule Mirouet*. It mourned Balzac's death as a great loss to the movement, but it took heart at his posthumous appearances at somnambulist séances (see II, 25–26; IV, 284–287; X, 59–60; XV, 74, 170).

may have read the physiological explanation of mesmeric "extase," a state that fascinated him, in Cabanis' *Rapports du physique et du moral de l'homme.* He studied Lavater's physiognomy and Dr. F. G. Gall's phrenology, which had been associated with mesmerism in a book by J. G. E. Oegger. The ideas of Swedenborg, Lavater, Gall, and possibly Cabanis thus blended in Balzac's description of the "imperceptible fluid, the basis of the phenomena of the human will, from which the passions, habits and the shape of the face and the skull result." But mesmerism provided the basic ingredient of this blend, for mesmerism had shaped the ideas of Lavater and Saint-Martin; and the mesmerist movement had evolved along the same lines as Balzac's own ideas—from extreme rationalism and even materialism to spiritualism. Thus it was essentially mesmerism that enabled Balzac's characters to see into one another's minds, to look through impenetrable objects, to explain water witching, to travel miraculously through space and time, and to consult ghosts. It intervened to save Pons' life and to form Mme. Cibot's plot in *Le Cousin Pons;* it separated and then reunited Marianine and Béringheld in *Le Centenaire;* it smote Raphaël with an "electric blow" of "scientific love" in *La Peau de chagrin;* it carried love between Sténie and Del Ryès in *Sténie;* and it lifted Lambert into a state of spiritual "harmony" in *Louis Lambert.*[20]

20. Balzac, *Ursule Mirouet,* Calmann Lévy ed. (Paris), pp. 82, 77; P.-J.-G. Cabanis, *Rapports du Physique et du Moral de l'homme . . .* 8 ed. (Paris, 1844), pp. 134–135 (the tenth member of the Society of Harmony was a "Cabanis" from Brive-la-Gaillarde; this was probably the philosopher, then a medical student, or his father, who died in Brive in 1786); Balzac, *La Peau de chagrin* (Paris, 1900), p. 151; Balzac, *Louis Lambert,* p. 211. On Balzac's introduction to occult science, see Bernard Guyon, *La Pensée politique et sociale de Balzac* (Paris, 1947), pp. 40–41 and 136–145. Swedenborgianism often was amalgamated with other doctrines in mesmerist theory, as one can see simply from the title of L.-A. Cahagnet's *Magnétisme: Encyclopédie magnétique spiritualiste, traitant spécialement de faits psychologiques, magie magnétique, swedenborgianisme, nécromancie, magie céleste, etc.* (Argenteuil, 1855).

Balzac could not have had a more appropriate or a more mesmerist escort for his final journey into the supernatural than Victor Hugo, who acted as pallbearer and eulogizer at his funeral. Mesmerism had prepared Balzac for the journey, for it had reinforced his religious faith and had brought him out of the eighteenth century by a route like that traveled by Dr. Minoret in *Ursule Mirouet* and indeed by most early nineteenth-century mesmerists. A somnambulist session upset the "Voltairian old age" (vieillesse voltairienne) of Dr. Minoret, an old-fashioned philosophe who had persecuted mesmerists before the Revolution, and prepared him for an "electric" shaft of grace. Through mesmerism, "the favorite science of Jesus," and also the philosophy of ancient Egypt, India, and Greece, Minoret learned "that a spiritual universe exists." The doctor turned Christian, abandoned his faith in Locke and Condillac, and took up the works of Swedenborg and Saint-Martin. Balzac might have added Hugo's works to the list, for they marked the high point of mesmerism's influence on spiritualist literature. A strong current of mesmerism flowed through Hugo's poems in company with the transmigrating souls, the hierarchy of invisible spirits, the primitive religions, and the other elements of spiritualism. Mesmerism occupied as proud a place in Hugo's "Préface philosophique" to *Les Misérables* as it had occupied in Balzac's Foreword to *La Comédie Humaine*. It demonstrated, according to Hugo, that "science, under the pretext of miraculousness, has abandoned its scientific duty, which is to get at the root of all things." Mesmerism led Hugo beyond science to a vision of "l'harmonie universelle," where sun, moon, and stars spun silently in an ocean of fluid. Hugo called it the "vital fluid," the essence of life and of the afterlife; for mesmerism brought him into the supernatural, the world that he longed to enter, not in order to satisfy metaphysical curiosity, but to regain contact with Léopoldine, his beloved, dead daughter. Paralyzed with grief, in exile on the Channel Islands, he seized desperately at the chance of communicating with Léopoldine, which was offered to him by Mme. de Girardin, the somnambulist colleague of Balzac and Gautier. The records of their séances show the broken poet exchanging verse with Shakespeare and Dante, receiving revolutionary advice from Jesus, and, in a pitiful moment, asking his dead daughter, "Do you see the suffering of those who love you?" (Vois-tu la souffrance de ceux qui t'aiment?) and being assured by her that it would soon end. The rational, scientific ideas of the eighteenth century could not contain the suffering of Hugo; he, like Dupont, fought off despair by retreating into poetry and spiritualism. Samuel Johnson had been able to save himself from despair in the mid-eighteenth century by invoking "celestial Wisdom"; Hugo also turned to religion in the mid-nineteenth century, but not to the orthodox Christianity that had died with the Enlightenment: he searched the skies with the help of science or, rather, "high science" (haute science):

> Pendant que l'astronome, inondé de rayons,
> Pèse un globe à travers des millions de lieues,
> Moi, je cherche autre chose en ce ciel vaste et pur.
> Mais que ce saphir sombre est un abîme obscur!
> On ne peut distinguer, la nuit, les robes bleues
> Des anges frissonnants qui glissent dans l'azur.[21]

---

21. Balzac, *Ursule Mirouet*, pp. 97–100, 75; Victor Hugo, "Préface Philosophique," in *Oeuvres romanesques complètes,* ed. Francis Bouvet (Paris, 1962), pp. 889, 879; *Chez Victor Hugo: Les tables tournantes de Jersey: procès-verbaux des séances présentés et commentés par Gustave Simon* (Paris, 1923), p. 34; Hugo, "Pendant que le marin, qui calcule et qui doute" in book 4 of *Les Contemplations,* Joseph Vianey ed. (Paris, 1922), pp. 377–378. The lines can be translated literally, "While the astronomer, inundated with rays,/Weighs a globe across millions of leagues,/I myself search for something else in that vast and pure sky./But what an obscure abyss is that dark sapphire!/One can not distinguish at night the blue gowns/Of the fluttering angels who slip through the

Animal magnetism had gone through several reincarnations since Mesmer announced its existence to Paris in 1778; by the time it had infiltrated *La Comédie Humaine* and *Les Misérables,* it had left the Enlightenment behind, in ruins.

---

azure." Hugo expressed his mesmerist convictions more explicitly but less beautifully in many other poems of *Les Contemplations.* For a general study of his mysticism, see Auguste Viatte, *Victor Hugo et les illuminés de son temps* (Montreal, 1942).

6. CONCLUSION

The mesmerism that lifted Victor Hugo's poetry into the supernatural would not have been recognized by the men who sat around the first mesmeric tubs and quoted the philosophes while congratulating one another on the victory that they had won for Reason. The first mesmerists had been mistaken in their glimpses of the future but not entirely wrong in the belief that their science would remake the world; for the mesmerism of the 1780's supplied much of the material with which Frenchmen rebuilt their views of the world after the Revolution, and these views, with all their ghosts and copulating planets, were as important to many of them as the first railroads. Thus, the mesmerist movement provides a guideline to the subtle transformation of popular attitudes during the periods generally labeled the Age of Reason and the Age of Romanticism; in fact, it has outlived those periods and survives to this day on the *grands boulevards* of Paris, where the occasional mesmerist still manipulates his fluid for a price. The modern mesmerists are a sadly declined and depopulated race, however, and Parisians now hurry past them without a curious glance.

Curiosity and the stronger passion for "the marvelous" consumed the Parisians of the 1780's and spirited a number of fads that provide valuable information about the attitudes of the reading public at that time. Worthy of study in themselves, these attitudes are especially important for understanding how radical ideas circulated in prerevolutionary France. From the elite who applauded Lavoisier's experiments in the Academy of Sciences to the Sunday strollers who paid 12 livres for a half-hour balloon ride above the Moulin de Javelle in Paris, Frenchmen burned with enthusiasm for the greatest fashion of the decade before 1787—science. Reports of scientific marvels filled the popular literature of the 1780's; they even filled the thoughts of Marat and Robespierre. How natural, then, for radicals to use the scientific vogue as a vehicle for the communication of their ideas. Even balloons could be made to carry radical messages. An unknown young commoner named Fontaine jumped into a Montgolfière just as it was taking off at Lyons on January 19, 1784, and reportedly said to the prince, the count, the knight of Saint Louis, and the other distinguished passengers who had refused him a place, "On earth I respected you, but here we are equals." Here was a deed to electrify the youth of France! Here was a statement of equality, published in a well-known newspaper, to ring in ears that had never heard of Rousseau's *Social Contract*.[1]

Mesmerism even surpassed balloon flights in arousing enthusiasm during the 1780's. By exploiting this enthusiasm, mesmerist propaganda, produced by radicals as extreme as Jacques-Pierre Brissot, played an important part in the obscure process by which radical ideas filtered down from treatises on political theory to the vulgar reading public. This public thrilled to the mysteries, scandals, and passionate polemics of mesmerism and generally ignored the *Social Contract*. Rousseau's abstruse treatise, unlike his other works, had no relevance to the apolitical interests of ordinary readers, while mesmerism had all the necessary ingredients of a pre-1789 cause célèbre. Although only a small minority of mesmerist pamphlets contained a political message, and these pamphlets failed to provoke much of an outcry among the regime's supporters, the mesmerist attacks on the abuses of French society did not lack force: they hit home, because they struck from within the popular and apolitical vogue of science. They hit hard enough to alarm the police, and the police failed to return the blows only because the Parlement of Paris rallied to the mesmerists' support. The Parlement's stand put it in contact with radical mesmerist pamphleteers, who later popularized its

1. *Journal de Bruxelles*, January 31, 1784, p. 228. On the commercial balloon flights, see *Courier de l'Europe*, November 16, 1784, p. 315.

attacks on the government during the prerevolutionary crisis of 1787–1788. The mesmerists' skirmish with the government in 1784 prepared for those attacks by uniting the antigovernment forces in the group that met at Kornmann's house after being expelled by the more genteel members of the Society of Universal Harmony. The Kornmann group represents the culmination of mesmerism's movement into politics, for the group's members campaigned vigorously against the Calonne and Brienne ministries. The resistance to the government was led in the Parlement by d'Eprémesnil and Duport, in the Notables by Lafayette, at the Bourse by Clavière, and among the reading public by Brissot, Carra, Gorsas, and Bergasse. It would take another book to analyze that campaign, however, as the issues of 1787–1788 were badly muddled: opposition to the government and support of the parlements could be interpreted as a sign of reactionary as well as of radical convictions.

Despite its vagueness, "radical" seems the best term to apply to the men who wanted to produce a fundamental change in French politics and society; it fits the mesmerists who expected their science to remake France and whose writings had the flavor of revolutionary propaganda. It does not fit the majority of mesmerists, the abbots and countesses and wealthy merchants whose attachment to Mesmer's tubs indicated only a dread of disease, of boredom, or of missing out on the most fashionable parlor game of the decade. The fashionable character of mesmerism helps explain the tone of life, the *moeurs,* as the French of the eighteenth century would put it, among the upper classes during the 1780's. Its radical character does not prove that the Ancien Régime was mined by a secret network of revolutionary cells like those imagined by the Abbé Barruel; it serves rather as an indication of how much that regime's foundation had been eroded by lack of faith among the literate elite. Lafayette, Brissot, Bergasse, and Carra might have found some other occasion for coordinating their attacks against the system. They certainly did not need mesmerist theory to be convinced of its evils. But when they were capable of reading a revolutionary message into Mesmer's Germanic gibberish, when they chose his tubs as a forum for demanding the transformation of French society, they bore witness to the depth of their discontent with the social order. It was this discontent, rather than any reform program, that set their ideas afire and provoked them to inflame the public.

Mesmerism appealed to radicals in two ways: it served as a weapon against the academic establishment that impeded, or seemed to impede, their own advancement, and it provided them with a "scientific" political theory. Not only did it offer a young revolutionary like Brissot an opportunity to associate himself with the latest scientific fashion, the most controversial issue of the decade, but it also aroused his innermost feelings, his ambition to climb to the pinnacle of French science and letters, and his hatred of the men at the top. Pinnacles are narrow by definition, but Brissot, Carra, and Marat interpreted the narrowness of the academic establishment in political terms. They regarded academicians as "despots" and "aristocrats" of philosophy, who oppressed those of inferior status and superior genius. Their hatred of oppression carried them from philosophy to politics with the outbreak of the Revolution, and it is the sole spark of life remaining in their dead discourses on the nature of fire or the best way to guide balloons. Marat, the prerevolutionary expert on those two topics, anticipated Marat the revolutionary in his demand for something like popular sovereignty in scientific matters. "If I must be judged, then let it be by an enlightened and impartial public: it is to its tribunal that I confidently appeal, to that supreme tribunal whose decrees the scientific bodies themselves are forced to respect." Mesmer met the attacks of academicians with the same defense: "It is to the public that I appeal." The names of Marat and Mesmer sound odd together, but they represent an important aspect of the radical movement of the 1780's. Mesmer's appeal, especially, reverberated up and down the grub streets of Paris, where countless unappreciated successors to Newton and Voltaire cursed the establishment from the squalor described by Mallet du Pan: "Paris is full of young men who take a little facility to be talent, of clerks, shop assistants, lawyers, soldiers, who make themselves into authors, die of hunger, even beg, and produce pamphlets." The frustrated ambitions of these men provided the thrust behind many revolutionary careers: a study of them might go far toward explaining the genesis of the revolutionary elite.[2]

It is the genesis of a revolutionary mood, the mood that took hold of many Frenchmen in the generation after the death of the great philosophes, that mesmerism helps explain. The literate French of the late 1780's tended to reject the cold rationalism of the midcentury in favor of a more exotic intellectual diet. They yearned for the supra-rational and the scientifically mysterious. They buried Voltaire and flocked to Mesmer. The most outspoken of them lacked the proper accent, the bon ton of the Enlightenment Fathers, for they refused to whittle away at abuses with witticisms. They would obliterate the social evils that limited access to positions of power and prestige, and so they embraced mesmerism, a cause that gave vent to their fascination with the supernatural, their crusading instincts, and their resentment of privilege. To those who had lost faith in the old system, mesmerism offered a new faith, a faith that marked the end of the Enlightenment, the advent of the Revolution, and the dawning of the nineteenth century.

---

2. J.-P. Marat, *Découvertes de M. Marat sur la lumière* . . . 2 ed. (London, 1780), p. 6; F. A. Mesmer, *Précis historique des faits relatifs au magnétisme animal* . . . (London, 1781), p. 40; *Mémoires et correspondance de Mallet du Pan, pour servir à l'histoire de la Révolution française, recueillis et mis en ordre par A. Sayous* (Paris, 1851), I, 130.

Mesmerism also appealed to some of the privileged, to men like Lafayette, Duport, and d'Esprémesnil, who flirted with ideas that undercut their exalted social position. These men championed mesmerism as a medicine of the common people, a science that would restore the healthy primitives of Rousseau and Court de Gébelin. Health would produce virtue, the virtue described by Rousseau and Montesquieu, and virtue would create harmony within the body politic as well as within individuals. Mesmerism would regenerate France by destroying "obstacles" to "universal harmony"; it would remedy the pernicious effects of the arts (another idea adapted from Rousseau) by restoring a "natural" society in which physico-moral laws of nature would drown aristocratic privileges and despotic government in a sea of mesmeric fluid. First to go, of course, would be the doctors. The program of the mesmerist revolution then became vague, but its central proposition remained clear: the elimination of doctors would set natural laws at work to root out all social abuses, for the despotism of doctors and their academic allies represented the last attempt of the old order to preserve itself against the forces of the true science of nature and society.

The radical mesmerists expressed their contemporaries' feeling that the Ancien Régime had decayed beyond the point of natural recovery. Major surgery was needed, and the court doctors could not be trusted to perform it. The mesmerists undertook the task, armed with their own medicine, and managed to inflict some deep wounds; but after the death of the old order, they saw that they had been united by a common desire for change, not by clearly defined objectives, and they turned on one another. D'Eprémesnil's parliamentary bias showed itself to be a reactionary program for the rule of the nobility of the robe; Bergasse withdrew in disillusionment from the National Assembly after the October days; Lafayette and Duport ruled France for a while as conservative constitutional monarchists only to be overcome by Brissot and Carra, who rose (or fell) into power with the Girondists; and Marat helped his former friends to the guillotine before his own murder, which meant the end of his wonderful fluids and the visions they all had shared.

BIBLIOGRAPHICAL NOTE
APPENDICES
INDEX

BIBLIOGRAPHICAL NOTE

Because the mesmerists considered their movement
to be of enormous historical importance, they recorded
it in great detail. Thousands of mesmeric cures, visions,
and philosophical speculations fill the fourteen quarto
volumes of about 1000 pages each in the mesmerist
collection of the Bibliothèque Nationale, 4° Tb 62.1. The
collection was assembled during the eighteenth century
(it was probably completed in 1787) and contains many
helpful manuscript notes, including an "Avertissement"
explaining its purpose: to document "les écarts de la
raison humaine." Despite its claim to be a "Recueil
général et complet de tous les écrits publiés pour et
contre le magnétisme animal," it lacks many important
mesmerist works and was supplemented in the preparation of this study by consulting the rich eighteenth-
century pamphlet collections of the British Museum.
There is a useful but incomplete bibliography of mesmerism by Alexis Dureau, *Notes bibliographiques pour
servir à l'histoire du magnétisme animal* . . . (Paris, 1869).

The manuscript sources consulted for this work
were:

PARIS: Archives Nationales, T 1620 (inventory of
Duport papers), and W 479 and F⁷ 4595 (Bergasse and the
Revolution).

Bibliothèque Nationale, fonds français, 6684 and
6687 (Hardy's journal), 1690 ("Recueil sur les médecins
et les chirurgiens" in the Joly de Fleury collection, containing letters from Mesmer and his followers), and
Cabinet des Estampes (topical cartoons, especially from
the Hennin and Vinck collections).

Bibliothèque de l'Institut de France, ms 883 (Condorcet papers).

Bibliothèque historique de la ville de Paris, ms série 84 and Collection Charavay, mss 811 and 813 (papers of the Parisian Société de l'Harmonie, incomplete).

VILLIERS, LOIR-ET-CHER: Château de Villiers (Bergasse papers).

AVIGNON: Bibliothèque municipale, mss 3059 and 3060 (Corberon papers).

ORLÉANS: Bibliothèque municipale, mss 1421 and 1423 (Lenoir papers).

LA ROCHELLE: Bibliothèque municipale, ms 358 (biographical sketch of Petiot and the letter printed in Appendix 2).

GRENOBLE: Bibliothèque municipale, mss R 1044 and N 1761 (Servan papers).

STRASBOURG: Archives de la ville, mss AA 2660 and 2662 (papers of the Préteur royal).

ZURICH: Zentralbibliothek, ms 149 (Lavater papers).

The principal pamphlets and other printed sources upon which this study is based have been cited in the footnotes, but a word about other works on mesmerism is in order here. Most were written by mesmerists. Any good library contains shelves of volumes, mostly published in the nineteenth century, purporting to reveal or refute occult systems of medicine or of communicating with spirits. They make interesting reading for a while, but their taste soon palls. The reader investigating the mesmerism of the 1780's would do well to skip these works and to go directly to the writings of Bergasse, Mesmer, and the other prominent mesmerists of that time. But he should not fail to consult the *Journal du magnétisme animal* . . . (Paris, 1852), which contains the only complete list of the 430 members of the Parisian Société de l'Harmonie. The list was compiled from the society's records and tallies with the incomplete collection of them in the Bibliothèque historique de la ville de Paris. The reader also might profit from the work by J. P. F. Deleuze, the last of the old school of mesmerists, *Histoire critique du magnétisme animal* (Paris, 1813); and if he is interested in an account of the movement by a modern mesmerist, he should consult Emil Schneider, *Der Animale Magnetismus, seine Geschichte und seine Beziehungen zur Heilkunst* (Zurich, 1950).

Works by nonmesmerists usually honor Mesmer as a misunderstood and sometimes heroic prophet of modern psychology. It may be that psychoanalysis developed from a line of occult scientists, linking Freud, Charcot, and Braid with Bertrand, Puységur, and Mesmer, just as chemistry emerged from alchemy; but Mesmer's reputation does not benefit from an examination of his financial dealings, nor from the disclosure that his doctoral thesis (written, to be sure, before his discovery of animal magnetism) was highly unoriginal, if not actually plagiarized (Frank Pattie, "Mesmer's Medical Dissertation and its Debt to Mead's De Imperio Solis ac Lunae," *Journal of the History of Medicine and Allied Sciences,* XI [1956], 275–287). There was probably as much of Cagliostro as of Freud in Mesmer's constitution, but the possibility that he was a charlatan need not worry the historian concerned with the movement rather than the man. The movement, however, has usually been treated as an episode in the history of medicine; thus: Rudolf Tischner, *Franz Anton Mesmer, Leben, Werk und Wirkungen* (Munich, 1928); Bernhard Milt, *Franz Anton Mesmer und Seine Beziehungen zur Schweiz: Magie und Heilkunde zu Lavaters Zeit* (Zurich, 1953); Margaret Goldsmith, *Franz Anton Mesmer: The History of an Idea* (London, 1934); D. M. Walmsley, *Anton Mesmer* (London, 1967); Ernest Bersot, *Mesmer et le magnétisme animal, les tables tournantes et les esprits,* 4 ed. (Paris, 1879); Jean Vinchon, *Mesmer et son secret* (Paris, 1936); and E. V. M. Louis, *Les Origines de la doctrine du magnétisme animal: Mesmer et la Société de l'Harmonie, thèse pour le doctorat en médecine* (Paris, 1898); actually, this last book contains very little information about the society. More useful are Louis Figuier, *Histoire du merveilleux dans les temps modernes,* 2 ed. (Paris, 1860), vol. III, and R. Lenoir, "Le mesmérisme et le système du monde," *Revue d'histoire de la philosophie,* I (1927), 192–219 and 294–321.

More useful still are works in the fertile field of eighteenth-century science, particularly the following: C. C. Gillispie, *The Edge of Objectivity: An Essay in the History of Scientific Ideas* (Princeton, 1960); Jacques Roger, *Les Sciences de la vie dans la pensée française du XVIIIe siècle* (Paris, 1963); I. B. Cohen, *Franklin and Newton* (Philadelphia, 1956); Daniel Mornet, *Les Sciences de la nature en France au XVIIIe siècle* (Paris, 1911); Philip Ritterbush, *Overtures to Biology: The Speculations of Eighteenth-Century Naturalists* (New Haven and London, 1964); Everett Mendelsohn, *Heat and Life: The Development of the Theory of Animal Heat* (Cambridge, Mass., 1964); Erik Nordenskiöld, *The History of Biology: A Survey,* tr. L. B. Eyre (New York, 1946); F. J. Cole, *Early Theories of Sexual Generation* (Oxford, 1930); Alexandre Koyré, *From the Closed World to the Infinite Universe* (Baltimore, 1957); Alexandre Koyré, *Newtonian Studies* (Cambridge, Mass., 1965); Abraham Wolf, *A History of Science, Technology and Philosophy in the Eighteenth Century* (London, 1952); J. H. White, *The History of the Phlogiston Theory* (London, 1932); Maurice Daumas, *Lavoisier, théoricien et expérimentateur . . .* (Paris, 1955); Hélène Metzger, *Les Doctrines chimiques en France du début du XVIIe à la fin du XVIIIe siècle* (Paris, 1925); Douglas Guthrie, *A History of Medicine* (London, 1945); *Buffon,* essays published by the Muséum National d'Histoire Naturelle (Paris, 1952); and P. F. Mottelay, *Biographical History of Electricity and Magnetism* (London, 1922). And most useful of all is browsing in the articles of the great *Encyclopédie* and, especially, eighteenth-century periodicals, both those on scientific subjects, like the *Journal de Physique* and the *Journal des Sçavans,* and those on general topics, like the *Journal de Paris, Mercure, Almanach des Muses, Année littéraire, Courier de l'Europe,* and *Journal de Bruxelles.* These offer information on the state of ideas on a vulgar level, the level that rarely finds treatment in conventional intellectual histories.

APPENDIX 1. MESMER'S PROPOSITIONS

Mesmer reduced his theory of animal magnetism to twenty-seven propositions, which he published at the end of his *Mémoire sur la découverte du magnétisme animal* (Geneva, 1779). The most important are the following:

1. Il existe une influence mutuelle entre les corps célestes, la terre et les corps animés.

2. Un fluide universellement répandu, et continué de manière à ne souffrir aucun vide, dont la subtilité ne permet aucune comparaison, et qui, de sa nature, est susceptible de recevoir, propager et communiquer toutes les impressions du mouvement, est le moyen de cette influence.

8. Le corps animal éprouve les effets alternatifs de cet agent; et c'est en s'insinuant dans la substance des nerfs, qu'il les affecte immédiatement.

9. Il se manifeste particulièrement dans le corps humain des propriétés analogues à celles de l'aimant; on y distingue des pôles également divers et opposés, qui peuvent être communiqués, changés, détruits et renforcés; le phénomène même de l'inclinaison y est observé.

10. La propriété du corps animal, qui le rend susceptible de l'influence des corps célestes, et de l'action réciproque de ceux qui l'environnent, manifestée par son analogie avec l'aimant, m'a déterminé à la nommer magnétisme animal.

21. Ce système fournira de nouveaux éclaircissements sur la nature du feu et de la lumière, ainsi que dans la théorie de l'attraction, du flux et reflux, de l'aimant et de l'électricité.

23. On reconnaîtra par les faits, d'après les règles pratiques que j'établirai, que ce principe peut guérir immédiatement les maladies des nerfs, et médiatement les autres.

APPENDIX 2. THE MILIEU OF AMATEUR SCIENTISTS IN PARIS

This description of the Parisian lycées and musées, which includes a reference to Jean-Louis Carra, comes from a letter written during a trip to Paris by La Villemarais, of the Academy of La Rochelle, to his colleague Seignette. It was copied from the manuscript in the Bibliothèque de la ville de La Rochelle and sent to the present writer by La Rochelle's most obliging librarian, Mlle. O. B. de Saint-Affrique.

PARIS, le 12 février 1783

... Les beaux esprits et les savants sont presqu'invisibles ici; quelques uns même ne reçoivent de visites qu'un jour de la semaine, comme les Ministres, et si on veut les voir il faut aller à leur audience publique. J'ai déjà entendu une partie des professeurs de physique et d'histoire naturelle—ceux qui ont le plus de mérite ont souvent des moyens si ingrats qu'on ne peut tirer aucun profit de leurs leçons, cependant les hommes, les femmes, de tout age, s'y portent en foule. J'allai, il y a huit jours, au fameux Musée, rue Sainte-Avoye, où M. Pilâtre de Rozier devait donner une récapitulation de tout ce qu'il avait enseigné depuis trois mois. Je fus introduit dans un assez beau cabinet, orné de fort beaux instruments de physique expérimentale—le milieu était occupé par une superbe machine électrique à deux plateaux, autour de laquelle un double rang de femmes, très parées, formait une enceinte qui occupait les trois quarts du cabinet; par derrière, dans les coins et jusque dans l'antichambre les hommes étaient entassés pêle-mêle; on entendait à peine le jeune professeur, qui doctement expliquait les premiers phénomènes de l'électricité, et très souvent appelait la machine à son secours; deux ou trois coups de ballon tirés à l'improvisé, des jets de lumière extraordinaires, et l'inflammation de la poudre à canon, jetèrent parfois la belle portion de l'assemblée dans un grand désordre, des voix charmantes poussèrent des cris aigus, mais tout fut rajusté par la présence d'esprit de M. de Rozier, qui nous assura qu'il n'y avait rien à craindre. Je vous envoie ci-joint le prospectus de ce Musée pour que vous en preniez une idée: vous verrez qu'il ne ressemble en rien à celui de M. Court de Gébelin, qui n'est qu'une société littéraire, une ombre imparfaite des académies, ou chaque membre lit ce qu'il a écrit sur tel sujet que bon lui semble. J'y fus encore jeudi dernier. M. Caillava, Président, lut la préface d'un ouvrage sur l'art dramatique. M. de St. Ange donna un morceau de sa traduction des Métamorphoses d'Ovide; M. du Carla, physicien qui n'est pas sans mérite, lut une très courte dissertation sur la lumière zodiacale; M. Carra en lut une autre beaucoup trop longue sur les vibrations *sonifiques* comparées aux vibrations *lucifiques,* enfin le cher M. Monnet nous donna je ne sais quoi sur certains petits osselets fossiles, qu'il a vus, je ne sais où; c'était écrit à peu près comme il parle. On lut encore des odes latines et françaises, des vers envoyés par des correspondants, des extraits de voyage; mais ce qui parut faire le plus de plaisir à l'assemblée, c'est un fragment de poésie imitative tiré d'un poème que M. Depiis se propose sans doute de faire imprimer: ce dernier morceau fut vivement applaudi. Après les lectures on donna, comme d'usage, un peu de musique. Il me reste à voir le Musée de M. de la Blancherie; je tâcherai d'y aller jeudi, si on ne donne pas un opéra de Gluck.

APPENDIX 3. THE SOCIÉTÉ DE L'HARMONIE UNIVERSELLE

The society's secret meetings took place in a vast room decorated with expensive tapestries and mirrors in the Hôtel de Coigny, rue Coq-Héron. Their character is best described by the Journal of the Baron de Corberon, the French chargé d'affaires in Russia from 1775–1780, who experimented with every form of mysticism and occultism he could find. The first part of his journal was published by L.-H. Labande, *Un diplomate français à la cour de Cathérine II, 1775–1780. Journal intime du Chev. de Corberon, chargé d'affaires de France en Russie,* 2 vols. (Paris, 1901). The excerpts from the remaining part of his journal, transcribed below, come from the Bibliothèque municipale d'Avignon, mss 3059 and 3060. After a preliminary interview with Mesmer and a special session for neophytes, Corberon was inducted into the society on April 5, 1784.

C'est aujourd'hui ... que j'ai été reçu chez Mesmer; c'est-à-dire membre de l'harmonie, car on a donné un nom et des formes de maçonnerie à ce qui n'en devait point avoir. Nous étions 48 environ de récipiendaires. Une grande salle au premier de l'ancien hôtel de Coigny, rue Coq-héron, était préparée à cet effet. Beaucoup de lumières souvent disposées par trois, éclairaient cette pièce. Un arrangement de sièges, de fauteuils, etc., tout donnait à cette assemblée un petit air de charlatanerie qui m'a déplu, je l'avoue, mais qui était peut-être nécessaire pour bien des gens ...

Au fond de cette salle il y avait une estrade derrière laquelle étaient assis les 3 président et vice-présidents; une table devant eux couverte d'un tapis rouge ainsi que les fauteuils. Mesmer au milieu, à sa droite M. de Chatelux, à sa gauche M. Duport, les 2 vice-présidents.

On a fait un petit discours qui ne [signifiait] pas grande chose sur l'importance de ce que nous allions faire, et toujours la forme maçonnique, les mailles pour faire silence etc. J'oubliais de dire qu'en avant de l'estrade des présidences, il y avait à droite un fauteuil et une table pour l'orateur, à gauche de même pour le secrétaire. Devant et dans le centre deux rangées de chaises, chacune de 12 ou 15 environ, autour duquel [sic] les 2 rangées de fauteuils, plutôt derrière qu'autour; et en troisième ligne des banquettes élevées sur lesquelles se sont placés les anciens reçus. En face de l'orateur et du secrétaire 2 autres tables et fauteuils auxquelles se sont placés 2 autres officiers de l'ordre qui figuraient là ce que sont dans les loges le premier et le deuxième surveillant. Voilà à-peu-près la figure ou plan de cette assemblée.

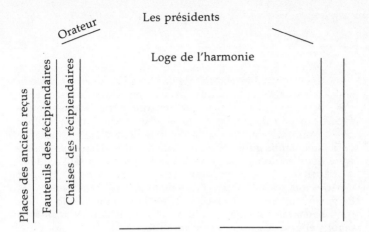

Loge de l'harmonie

Il y avait sur une glace derrière les présidents un tableau symbolique et aux deux côtés, c'est-à-dire au-dessus de l'orateur et de son pendant, un tableau écrit à la main qui marque ce que c'est que le magnétisme animal, son application par division et subdivisions.

[After a speech by the orator, Bergasse] . . . Nous avons tous levé la main et passé ensuite à tour de rôle au banc des présidents où nous avons reçu debout le signe de l'attouchement.

After his initiation, Corberon attended eleven indoctrination sessions, whose character may be judged by the following excerpts from his journal:

April 7: Nous étions tous autour d'une grande table d'un carré qui pouvait contenir une trentaine de personnes. Une planche de bois noirci propre à tracer des lignes occupait le milieu de cette table; elle est là pour tracer des figures analogues à la démonstration. Un ou deux bateaux de papier y est aussi, l'un rempli de boules de cire comme des balles de pistolet, l'autre de limaille de fer. Il y a aussi des cartons sur lesquels sont dessinés des figures de petites boules comme celles de cire rangées dans différents ordres: ces desseins sont relatifs aux démonstrations de la matière dont les boules de cire ou leur figure représentent des atomes ou des globules de matière. Des bougies, du papier, de l'encre, garnissent le reste de la table.

Mesmer est placé dans le milieu d'une des grandes faces de la table. Bergasse, orateur de la loge et démonstrateur à la leçon, est vis-à-vis de lui à l'autre face de cette même table. Armé d'une verge de cuivre ou d'or, qui n'est pas celle de Moïse, il a pris la parole . . .

Il y a dans nos assemblées d'instruction un inconvénient, c'est que le véritable maître, Mesmer, ne possède pas assez la langue française pour faire l'instruction et en conséquence c'est Bergasse, qui a de la facilité, qui parle. Mais, comme avec beaucoup d'opinion de lui-même, il a moins de science que de jargon, il délaie ce qu'il sait et revient avec complaisance là-dessus, tandis qu'il coule rapidement sur les choses abstraites et ne nous en donne pas une idée nette, précise et satisfaisante.

April 9: . . . Dans le courant de cette instruction où Mesmer a parlé plus qu'aux autres j'ai remarqué avec déplaisance que Bergasse l'interrompait avec l'air de la supériorité. Je trouve qu'il abuse de l'avantage qu'il a sur l'autrichien de manier la parole, et cela m'a indisposé contre lui.

April 12: . . . Ce Bergasse est sur le point de rompre avec Mesmer, et ce n'est pas, m'a-t-on dit, la première fois . . . En commençant la leçon Bergasse nous a annoncé que ce serait la dernière qu'il ferait d'un ton à faire penser qu'il y avait des raisons de mécontentement particulier, plus que des affaires qui l'en empêchaient. Le Chevalier Delfino, ambassadeur de Venise, qui était à côté de moi, en prit la même opinion, et me dit qu'il, . . . lui Bergasse, eut déjà la même idée de quitter la société par de semblables raisons d'amour-propre et de domination qui avaient fait naître des disputes assez vives avec le Comte Maxime Puységur, qui fera probablement l'instruction à sa place.

Corberon reported that Puységur replaced Bergasse on April 14 but did a poor job; by April 19 Bergasse had agreed to continue the lessons. Corberon discontinued the journal after his eleventh lesson, on April 30. When he took it up again, in November, he had lapsed in his mesmerist activities and had become involved with a man called Ruer, who claimed to possess the philosopher's stone and to be a successor of Solomon.

APPENDIX 4. BERGASSE'S LECTURES ON MESMERISM

These excerpts come from a lecture by Bergasse entitled "Idées générales sur le système du monde et l'accord des lois physiques et morales dans la nature," delivered on July 10, 1785, apparently in his public course on mesmerism following the schism in the Société de l'Harmonie. The original, in Bergasse's hand, is in his papers at the Château de Villiers, Villiers, Loir-et-Cher.

[Proposition] 70. De même que toutes les organisations font involontairement effort pour parvenir à l'équilibre physique entre elles, toutes les intelligences et toutes les volontés font involontairement effort pour parvenir à l'équilibre morale entre elles.

81. On pourrait appeler magnétisme moral artificiel toute théorie de moyens inventés pour produire entre les êtres intelligents une harmonie et une réciprocité d'affections et d'habitudes. A cette théorie appartiennent les institutions politiques et les divers formes d'éducation imaginées chez les différents peuples pour assurer la paix et la bonheur de la société.

82. On pourrait appeler électricité morale artificielle l'effort coupable que font un ou plusieurs individus pour détourner les affections et les habitudes qui les unissent à leurs semblables et les accumuler sur eux-mêmes.

86. De même que connaître la loi, d'après laquelle s'exerce le magnétisme physique universel et la théorie des procédés qui peuvent développer ou accroître l'énergie de cette loi est l'objet de l'art de préserver et de guérir ou de la médecine; de même aussi connaître la loi morale universelle d'après laquelle est produite l'harmonie des êtres intelligents et déterminer dans toutes les circonstances données, les institutions, les coûtumes, les préjugés qui peuvent développer ou accroître l'énergie de cette loi est l'objet de l'art de conduire et de gouverner ou de la législation.

87. Parce que, comme je viens de dire, les lois physiques et morales du monde, sont tellement ordonnées entre elles qu'appartenant à un seul plan, elles se terminent à un seul résultat,

tout ce qui dans un être organisé et intelligent blesse les lois morales doit nuire au développement des lois physiques, tout ce qui dans un être organisé et intelligent empêche ou détourne l'action des lois physiques doit affaiblir ou rendre plus difficile l'action des lois morales.

90. L'homme considéré comme un être moral est bon lorsque rien n'interrompt les affections et les habitudes qui le font tendre à l'équilibre moral avec lui-même et avec ses semblables.

105. Rien ne prouve plus l'existence d'une intelligence souveraine qui modère tout dans l'univers et ne donne une idée plus sublime de sa sagesse, que la combinaison profonde et le parfait accord des lois physiques et morales par lesquelles le même univers est gouverné.

Bergasse made the following remarks in a speech to the Société de l'Harmonie in 1783. The text, written in his hand and read during a meeting for the initiation of new members, was reprinted with extensive changes by Bergasse in *Discours et fragments de M. Bergasse* (Paris, 1808). The changes made it seem much less Rousseauist and deistic than the original in his papers at Villiers, from which the following excerpts were taken.

La Nature ne s'est évidemment proposée dans le développement de ses lois que de maintenir entre les êtres prodigieusement variés que l'immensité de son système embrasse, une constante et durable harmonie.

. . . Le bien sera pour vous tout ce qui est dans l'harmonie générale des êtres, le mal tout ce qui trouble cette harmonie . . . Vous apprendrez que cette justice n'est autre chose que cette grande énergie de la Nature qui rétablit par un mouvement général l'harmonie des êtres que des mouvements particuliers ont troublés quelques instants.

[The conscience is] . . . un organe véritable, un organe d'une sensibilité infinie qui s'unit par des fibres aussi nombreuses que déliées à tous les points de l'univers . . . C'est par cet organe que nous nous mettons en harmonie avec la nature, comme c'est par les autres que nous entretenons notre propre harmonie . . . Si dans un être malade l'organe de la conscience souffre, le rétablissement parfait des organes ordinaires est impossible; et vous arriverez ainsi à cette idée lumineuse et première, qu'il faut être bon pour être absolument sain . . . La pensée du méchant est un obstacle à l'action conservatrice de la nature . . . De là . . . une morale émanée de la

physique générale du monde . . . De là des règles simples pour
juger les institutions auxquelles nous sommes asservis, des
principes certains pour constituer la législation qui convient
à l'homme dans toutes les circonstances données, des lumières
imprévues sur la législation des crimes, législation dont les
idées premières n'ont pas encore été seulement aperçues,
d'autres moeurs parce qu'il nous faut d'autres lois, des moeurs
douces parce qu'elles ne naîtront pas de nos préjugés mais de
nos penchants, des moeurs faciles parce que peu de choses
sont défendues à l'homme de la nature, des moeurs sévères,
néanmoins, parce que la nature ne défend rien en vain à l'homme
qui reconnaît son empire.

APPENDIX 5. THE EMBLEM AND TEXTBOOK OF THE SOCIÉTÉS DE L'HARMONIE

The Societies' emblem shows their view of the physico-moral laws of nature, and their notebook, written by Bergasse, shows their use of symbols, which they generally considered as magic hieroglyphics, capable of communicating primitive truths. Both come from the mesmerist collection of the Bibliothèque Nationale, 4° Tb 62.

DEVISE des Sociétés de l'HARMONIE.

OBJET GÉNÉRAL.

Contemplation de l'harmonie de l'univers.
Connoissance des loix de la nature.

───────────────

Rapport et influence
de tous les êtres.
Physique universelle.

Rapport et influence de
toutes les actions.
Justice universelle.

OBJET PARTICULIER.

L'Homme.

Son Education.
Sa Conservation.

Législation.
Justice.

OBJET PRATIQUE.

Enseigner, maintenir et propager les principes.

De la Conservation.

De la Justice. { Sûreté.
Liberté.
Propriété.

De l'Education.

De la Médecine

ou de l'art de

guérir.

Des Vertus sociales. { Humanité.
Modération.
Frugalité.
Bienveillance.
Honnêteté.
Exactitude
dans les
procédés.
Sécurité.
Véracité.
Générosité.

Combattre les erreurs.

Empêcher l'injustice.

───────────────

(O) *En cet endroit, est placé un cartouche ovale*

s'élancent vers les autres et reciproquement. mais on sçait que tout 目 exis-
tant dans un = obeit au ⊗ de ce =

Donc si le = qui s'élance du 目 A.
se meut vers le 目 B. ⊗ reciproquement
les 目 A et B doivent tendre l'un vers
l'autre

Donc il y a une ⟍ mutuelle entre
tous les 目 Celestes.

39. La ⟍ des 目 Celestes est en raison
de leurs ◠; C'est a dire que si le 目 A
a plus de ◠ ou de ‖ que le 目 B.
il attire plus le 目 B qu'il n'en est at-
tiré, car on à vû que la rapidité des
➤ dans les quels les 目 sont plongés
est en raison de la ◠ ou de la ‖
des 目 (Fig: 37.)

40. La ⟍ des 目 Celestes est en raison de
leur distance c'est a dire que plus les
目 A et B (Fig: 38.) sont distans l'un de
l'autre et moins il s'attirent.

Car plus un 目 est éloigné d'un autre
corps et moins les ➤ qui sortent du premier pour entrer dans le second sont ⊙ convergents

Mais moins les ➤ sont ⊙ et moins
ils sont rapides, moins ils sont rapides et moins grande est la Célérité
avec laquelle ils entrainent les 目 qui
leur obeissent,

Donc plus les 目 sont eloignés et moins
ils s'attirent

Donc l' ⟍ des 目 Celestes est en raison de leur distance

41. La ⟍ des 目 Celestes s'exercesur toutes les parties qui les constituent; c'est
a dire que les parties d'un 目 tendent
chacune vers les parties d'un autre
目 et reciproquement, car comme il
ne peut y avoir de vuide dans la ∞
si un ∴ du 目 A tend vers B il faut
que cet ∴ tende a etre remplacé par
l' ∴ qui le fuit et ainsi successivement (Fig: 39.)

42. La ⟍ des 目 Celestes est plus dire-
cte entre les parties de leurs surfaces
qui se regardent qu'entre les parties
de leurs surfaces qui sont opposées,

Car dans le 目 A. les ➤ qui sortent
de la surface d d d sont plus direct vers le 目 B que les ➤ qui sortent de la surface d e d, (Fig: 40.)

43. Les 目 Celestes en tournant sur leur axe
s'opposent toujours la moitié de leurs surfaces

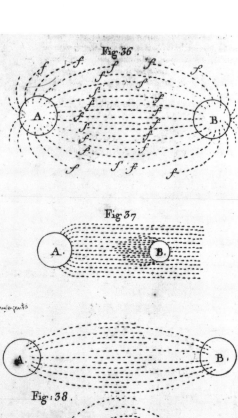

Fig: 36

Fig: 37

Fig: 38

tendance

Fig: 39

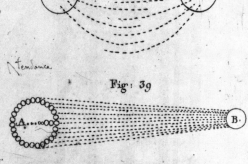

188

APPENDIX 6. AN ANTIMESMERIST VIEW

Condorcet entitled this essay "Raisons qui m'ont empêché jusqu'ici de croire au magnétisme animal." He probably wrote it in late 1784 or 1785 but never published it. It is in his papers at the Bibliothèque de l'Institut de France, ms 883, fol. 231–247.

Je respecte beaucoup les hommes distingués qui ont acheté le secret de M. Mesmer, parce qu'ils y croyaient d'avance, et qui ont continué d'y croire.

Mais Bodin croyait aux sorciers. L'imposture grossière des vampires attestée par une foule de témoins a eu pour historien le savant Dom Calmet. Jacques Aymar a eu des partisans illustres; la poudre du chevalier Digby a fait des prodiges sur des malades de tous les états. On est étonné des noms qu'on rencontre au bas des miracles de St. Médard. De nos jours on a cru à Parangue qui *voyait* l'eau à travers la terre, ce qui est un véritable miracle. Parmi les prosélites de Swedenborg on trouve des hommes instruits, occupant des places honorables, et raisonnables sur toute autre chose.

Les seuls témoins qu'on doive croire sur les faits extraordinaires sont ceux qui en sont les juges compétents. Il [existe], dit-on, un fluide universel dont les effets s'étendent depuis les astres les plus éloignés jusqu'à la terre. Eh bien, je n'y puis croire que sur l'autorité des physiciens. Ce fluide agit sur le corps humain. J'exige alors que ces physiciens joignent de la philosophie à leurs connaissances, parce que je dois me défier alors de l'imagination et de l'imposture. Ce fluide guérit les malades sans les toucher ou en les touchant; alors j'ai besoin que les médecins m'attestent la maladie et la guérison.

Mais le magnétisme animal a été admiré, employé par des physiciens ou des médecins. J'en conviens, mais il s'agit de me déterminer à croire sur une autorité; cela est dur pour la raison humaine. Ainsi je n'entends point par physicien ou par médecin un homme qui a fait des livres de physique ou qui a été reçu docteur dans quelque faculté. J'entends un homme qui, avant qu'il fut question du magnétisme, jouissait en France, en Europe même, d'une réputation bien établie. Voilà l'espèce de témoignage qu'il me faut pour croire un fait extraordinaire de physique ou de médecine.

Mais il faut encore que ce témoignage ne soit pas balancé par des témoignages contraires, à égalité de mérite et d'autorité. Un seul homme qui, admis à voir les mêmes faits, ou ne les voit pas ou n'y voit point le merveilleux qu'on y veut voir, balancera ceux qui auront vu.

Parce que la circonspection qui ne voit point trompe rarement et que l'enthousiasme qui veut croire trompe souvent.

D'après ces principes, on voit qu'il est impossible de croire au magnétisme animal, soit de M. Deslon, soit de M. Mesmer.

Examinons maintenant si, malgré la sainteté du secret, ces messieurs n'en ont pas assez dit ou assez laissé voir pour ôter toute espèce de motif de croire.

C'est l'imagination qui seule produit les effets attribués au magnétisme: qui me l'a dit? M. Mesmer lui-même et ses partisans, qui ont employé ouvertement tous les moyens connus pour exciter l'imagination: appareil merveilleux, postures bizarres ou contraintes, langage extraordinaire, réunion d'un grand nombre d'individus, des attouchements légers qui, dans des individus sensibles, produisent un effet qui les étonne et réveille l'activité de leur imagination.

L'approche du doigt produit même à une petite distance une sensation [illegible word] et fugitive qui devient un léger chatouillement lorsqu'on a une forte attention; [une] heureuse crédulité et l'imagination se chargent du reste. Des femmes vapoureuses sont magnétisées par des hommes, et il n'y a point de médecin éclairé, de physicien instruit qui ne sache combien il en peut résulter de choses merveilleuses, en supposant même dans les magnétiseurs l'innocence la plus complète.

Quelques personnes ont osé parler de charlatanisme, mais ces malades soumis à la volonté du magnétiseur, les cataleptiques qui n'en voient que mieux quand ils ont perdu la vue, ces malades qui devinent les maladies, tout cela n'a-t-il point la plus grande ressemblance aux fameuses histoires de démoniaques dont les livres sont pleins? Nicole de Vervins, Marthe Brossier, les Urselines de Loudun n'ont pas fait de choses moins merveilleuses.

Les raisonnements des magnétiseurs contre les préjugés des savants, ne sont-ils pas absolument les mêmes que ceux des charlatans les plus célèbres? L'exemple le plus frappant de l'opposition aux vérités physiques ou médicales est celui de [Harvey?]. On a remarqué qu'aucun médecin agé de quarante ans lors de sa découverte ne consentit à la croire. Mais un grand nombre de physiciens y crurent sans peine. L'exemple de Newton ne prouverait rien ici; personne ne nia ses découvertes. On persista seulement à vouloir les expliquer par des tourbillons; et on ne citera pas une seule découverte qui n'ait été reconnue en très peu de temps par la pluralité des savants;

et pas une des prétendues découvertes rejetée par eux qui n'ait été reconnue pour une chimère.

La manière dont les magnétiseurs défendent leur doctrine me paraît encore un violent préjugé contre eux. Par exemple, ils parlent de fluide magnétique, et ils ignorent que l'existence de ce fluide est bien loin d'être généralement reconnue. Ils donnent l'influence de la lune sur le corps humain pour une vérité avouée, et ni cette influence, ni les faits sur lesquels ils l'appuient ne sont admis. Ils comparent cette influence à l'action qui produit les marées, et ils ignorent que cette action a été soumise au calcul et qu'il résulte de ce calcul que cette action est nulle.

Parmi les personnes qui ont des secrets, les unes avouent franchement qu'elles les gardent pour s'enrichir; si cela n'est pas noble, cela n'est pas injuste: et, en vérité, l'exacte justice est si rare, et si on l'observait, le genre humain se trouverait si bien qu'on ferait fort bien de ne rien exiger de plus des hommes, du moins de sitôt.

Les autres disent qu'il y aurait du danger à révéler leur secret. Quelques uns le conservent pour que les étrangers, les ennemis de leur pays n'en profitent point. Ces derniers motifs sont suspects. Toutes les fois qu'un homme fait une chose utile à ses intérêts, il peut s'ouvrir à ses amis sur les motifs plus nobles qui peuvent l'inspirer, mais il ne doit jamais les dire au public, qui ne peut le croire.

D'ailleurs, comment ce secret si utile serait-il dangereux, s'il était connu? Ne l'est-il pas davantage en restant secret? S'il est public, ne trouvera-t-on pas les moyens de s'en défendre? Supposez la poudre à canon connue d'une seule nation, n'aurait-elle pas réduit toutes les autres à l'esclavage; les possesseurs du secret, ne seraient-ils pas les maîtres absolus de leur nation? Est-il possible de garder ce secret et cependant de le répandre assez pour qu'il soit utile?

Comme M. Mesmer est mécontent des académies, nous prendrons la liberté de raconter ici une petite anecdote. Un homme qui avait trouvé la quadrature du cercle se plaignait qu'on ne voulut pas l'examiner. "Mais," lui dit un académicien, "Ces examens font perdre inutilement beaucoup de temps." "Cela est bon pour les autres," dit le quadrateur, "N'examinez que la mienne; elle est seule bonne."

M. Mesmer veut-il que les gens sans préjugés croient à la réalité de son agent, ou veut-il ne persuader que ses malades?

S'il veut convaincre les gens sans préjugés, que son cabinet soit ouvert aux physiciens, que là, sans malades et n'ayant pour témoins que ceux qui ont bien voulu s'y rendre, il fasse des expériences bien simples, bien convaincantes; peu à peu il verra arriver successivement chez lui tous les hommes éclairés selon qu'ils sont plus ou moins disposés à croire. Il entendra leurs objections, il trouvera les moyens de les détruire.

Ne veut-il persuader que les malades? Il n'a rien à faire que ce qu'il a fait.

J'en demande pardon à M. Mesmer, je n'ai jamais cru, ni aux grandes découvertes qu'on garde dans son portefeuille, ni aux inventions dont on ne s'empresse point de prouver la réalité, ni aux complots des savants contre les nouvelles découvertes. Messieurs les inventeurs, si vous vous défiez de leur zéle pour la vérité, croyez au moins à leur orgeuil; ils ne demanderont pas mieux que de connaître ce que vous avez découvert, et ils ne douteront pas d'en tirer bientôt plus de vérités que vous-même.

APPENDIX 7. FRENCH PASSAGES TRANSLATED IN THE TEXT

Because the quotations in the text come, for the most part, from obscure sources and because it would be a pity for the reader to miss the flavor of the French, they are given here as they appeared in the original versions, with spelling modernized.

Page 13   On suppose que la nuit du songe de la dame d'Aiguemerre était une nuit d'été, que sa fenêtre était ouverte, son lit exposé au couchant, sa couverture en désordre et que le zéphyr du sud-ouest, dûment imprégné de molécules organiques de foetus humains, d'embryons flottants, l'avait fécondée.

Page 16   C'est sur les choses qu'on ne peut ni voir, ni palper, qu'il est important de se tenir en garde contre les écarts de l'imagination.

Page 17   Il a dû en coûter pour convenir que de l'eau ne fût pas de l'eau mais bien de l'air . . . Nous avons un élément de moins.

Page 18   Les poumons sont dans l'homme et dans les animaux la machine électrique par leur mouvement continuel, en séparant de l'air le feu, lequel s'insinue dans le sang et se porte, par ce moyen, au cerveau qui le distribue, l'impulse et en forme les esprits animaux qui circulent dans les nerfs pour tous les mouvements volontaires et involontaires.

Page 20   Il est impossible de rendre ce moment; les femmes en pleurs, tout le peuple levant les mains au ciel et gardant un silence profond; les voyageurs, le corps en dehors de la galerie, saluant et poussant des cris de joie. On les suit des yeux, on les appelle comme s'ils pouvaient entendre, et au sentiment d'effroi succède celui de l'admiration; on ne disait autre chose, sinon, "Grand Dieu que c'est beau"; grande musique militaire se faisait entendre, des boîtes annonçaient leur gloire.

Page 22   Ce furent quelques ouvriers mécontents d'avoir perdu leur journée et de n'avoir rien vu.

les dieux de l'antiquité porter sur des nuages; les fables se sont réalisées par les prodiges de la physique.

Les découvertes incroyables qui se multiplient depuis dix ans . . . les phénomènes de l'électricité approfondis, la transformation des éléments, les airs décomposés et connus, les rayons du soleil condensés, l'air que l'audace humaine ose parcourir, mille autres phénomènes enfin ont prodigieusement étendu la sphère de nos connaissances. Qui sait jusqu'où nous pouvons aller? Quel mortel oserait proscrire des bornes à l'esprit humain . . . ?

Page 24   L'amour du merveilleux nous séduit donc toujours; parce que, sentant confusément combien nous ignorons les forces de la nature, tout ce qui nous conduit à quelques découvertes en ce genre est reçu avec transport.

Dans tous nos cercles, dans tous nos soupers, aux toilettes de nos jolies femmes, comme dans nos lycées académiques, il n'est plus question que d'expériences, d'air atmosphérique, de gaz inflammable, de chars volants, de voyages aériens.

Page 26   Depuis que le goût des sciences a commencé à se répandre parmi nous, on a vu le public s'occuper successivement de physique, d'histoire naturelle, de chimie; et non seulement s'intéresser à leurs progrès, mais encore se livrer avec ardeur à leur étude: il se porte en foule aux écoles où elles sont enseignées; il s'empresse de lire les ouvrages dont elles sont le sujet; il recueille avec avidité tout ce qui lui en rappelle le souvenir; et il y a peu de personnes riches chez lesquelles on ne trouve quelques uns des instruments propres à ces sciences utiles.

aujourd'hui surtout que l'on cherche avec empressement tout ce qui a rapport à quelque découverte.

Page 27   On n'a plus pour la littérature qu'une froide estime qui approche de l'indifférence, tandis que les sciences . . . excitent un enthousiasme universel. La physique, la chimie, l'histoire naturelle sont devenues des passions.

Page 28   Lorsque des phénomènes visibles et frappants
          dépendent d'une cause insensible et inconnue,
          l'esprit humain, toujours porté au merveilleux,
          attribue naturellement ces effets à une cause
          chimérique.

          car je n'aime les vers que lorsqu'ils habillent un
          peu de physique ou de métaphysique.

Page 32   une belle occasion ... pour les naturalistes des
          deux mondes.

          Ces expériences ont tellement renversé les têtes
          faibles, qu'il n'est pas de jour sans projet plus ou
          moins extravagant, que l'on cite et que l'on accrédite.

Page 33   Des remèdes secrets de toute espèce se distribuent
          journellement, malgré la rigueur des défenses.

          philosophes hermétiques, cabalistiques, théosophes,
          propagant avec fanatisme toutes les anciennes
          absurdités de la théurgie, de la divination, de
          l'astrologie etc.

Page 38   ce langage sentimental qui nous fait communiquer
          nos pensées d'un pôle à l'autre.

          Rien n'est plus lumineux: c'est le vrai système de
          l'univers, le mobile de toutes choses.

          la physique prendrait partout la place de la magie.

          Au-dessus de la science est la magie, parce que
          celle-ci est une suite de l'autre, non comme effet,
          mais comme perfection de la science.

Page 40   une épidémie qui a gagné toute la France.

          Hommes, femmes, enfants, tout s'en mêle, tout
          magnétise.

          Le magnétisme occupe toutes les têtes. On est
          étourdi de ses prodiges, et si l'on se permet de
          douter encore des effets ... on n'ose plus nier au
          moins son existence.

          Le grand objet des entretiens de la capitale est
          toujours le magnétisme animal.

          on ne s'occupe que du magnétisme animal ...

Page 42   Il [Pilâtre] fut sourd à ma voix, et, comme un autre
          Cassandre, je criai dans le désert.

Page 55   Enfin, le célèbre auteur de la découverte du mag-
           nétisme animal a fait pour l'amour, ce que Newton
           fit pour le système du monde.

           démon dont je suis possédé; c'est ce coquin de
           Mesmer qui m'a ensorcelé.

Page 59   Aucun événement, pas même la Révolution, ne
           m'a laissé des lumières aussi vives que le mag-
           nétisme.

Page 60   Quant à l'électricité, j'ai une machine électrique
           qui m'amuse extrêmement tous ces jours; mais
           elle m'étonne bien davantage; jamais les effets du
           magnétisme ne m'ont autant frappé: si quelque
           chose achève de me confirmer l'existence d'un fluide
           universel, agent unique par les diverses modifica-
           tions de tant de phénomènes divers, ce sera ma
           machine électrique. Elle me parle le même langage
           que Mesmer sur la nature, et je l'écoute avec ravisse-
           ment.

           Car enfin qui sommes-nous, Monsieur, dans nos
           sentiments les plus exquis, comme dans nos plus
           vastes pensées, qui sommes-nous sinon une orgue
           plus ou moins admirable, composée de plus ou
           moins de jeux, mais dont le soufflet ne fut et ne sera
           jamais ni dans la glande pinéale de Descartes, ni
           dans la substance médullaire de la (illegible name),
           ni dans le diaphragme où l'ont placé certains
           rêveurs, mais dans le principe même qui meut
           tout l'univers. L'homme avec sa liberté ne marche
           qu'à la cadence de toute la nature, et toute la nature
           ne marche qu'à celle d'une cause unique; et quelle
           est cette cause unique sinon un fluide vraiment
           universel et qui pénètre la nature entière?

Page 62   . . . sera bientôt la seule médecine universelle.

           Jamais le tombeau de Saint Médard n'attira plus de
           monde et n'opéra des choses plus extraordinaires,
           que le mesmérisme. Il mérite enfin l'attention du
           gouvernement.

Page 65   cet arme d'un effet si sûr parmi nous.

           Magistrat, mais élève de M. Mesmer, si ma position
           personelle ne me permet plus de lui prêter directe-

ment le secours des lois, au moins lui dois-je, au nom de l'humanité, sur sa personne et sur sa découverte, un témoignage public de mon admiration et de ma reconnaissance, et je le donne.

Page 66   Elle résiste même aux traits les plus sanglants du ridicule. Si la capitale s'égaie des scènes vraiment très comiques du baquet, la province les a prises au sérieux: là sont les adeptes vraiment chauds.

Vous ne sauriez croire quels progrès rapides fait dans cette ville le magnétisme. Tout le monde s'en mêle.

Page 67   J'ai employé beaucoup de moyens pour être instruit . . . et j'ai acquis la conviction non seulement de l'existence mais de l'utilité de cet agent; et comme je suis animé du désir de procurer à notre bonne ville tous les avantages possibles, j'ai conçu à cet égard quelques vues que je vous communiquerai quand elles seront un peu digérées.

Page 70   Jetez, mes frères, les yeux sur le tableau harmonique de l'Ordre, qui couvre ce mystérieux baquet. C'est la Table Isiaque, une des antiquités des plus remarquables, où le mesmérisme se voit dans tout son jour, dans l'écriture symbolique de nos premiers pères en magnétisme animal et dont les seuls mesmériens ont la clef.

Il est certain que jamais les rose-croix, les adeptes, les prophètes et tout ce qui s'y rapporte, ne furent aussi nombreux, aussi écoutés. La conversation roule presque uniquement sur ces matières; elles occupent toutes les têtes; elles frappent toutes les imaginations . . . En regardant autour de nous, nous ne voyons que des sorciers, des adeptes, des nécromanciens et des prophètes. Chacun a le sien, sur lequel il compte.

Page 73   des personnes de tous les rangs, unies par le même lien.

Que la fierté des gens de haut rang soit choquée du mélange d'états et de conditions que l'on trouve chez moi cela ne m'étonne pas; mais je n'y sais rien. Mon humanité est de tous les rangs.

Les portes se ferment; on se place par ordre de souscription; et le petit bourgeois qui se croit pour un moment l'égal d'un cordon bleu, oublie ce que va lui coûter un siège de velours cramoisi bordé de l'or.

48 personnes, parmi lesquelles on compte 18 gentilshommes presque tous d'un rang éminent; 2 chevaliers de Malte; un avocat d'un mérite rare; 4 médecins; 2 chirurgiens, 7 à 8 banquiers ou négociants ou qui l'ont été; 2 ecclésiastiques; 3 moines.

Page 74   respect aveugle qui est dû au gouvernement: n'avons-nous pas dit que tout action, même toute pensée qui tend à troubler l'ordre de la société, était contraire à l'harmonie de la nature . . .

seigneur du château, sans apprêt, comme sans inquiétude ne paraît que pour maintenir l'ordre et recevoir l'hommage.

Page 76   On me demanda des règlements pour cette société, à laquelle on donna d'abord, bien malgré moi, la ridicule dénomination de *loge*.

Page 77   il y a bien des aimables de Paris qui aimeraient autant *Bergassiser* que *mesmériser*.

Page 78   J'ai renversé toutes les bases de son système et j'ai élevé sur les ruines de ce système un édifice, je crois, beaucoup plus vaste et plus solidement construit.

la morale universelle, sur les principes de la législation, sur l'éducation, les moeurs, les arts etc.

Page 79   Bergasse ne me cacha pas qu'en élevant un autel au magnétisme, il n'avait en vue que d'en élever un à la liberté."Le temps est arrivé, me disait-il, où la France a besoin d'une révolution. Mais vouloir l'opérer ouvertement, c'est vouloir échouer; il faut, pour réussir, s'envelopper du mystère; il faut réunir les hommes sous prétexte d'expériences physiques, mais, dans la vérité, pour renverser le despotisme." Ce fut dans cette vue qu'il forma dans la maison de Kornmann, où il demeurait, une société composée des hommes qui annonçaient leur goût pour les innovations politiques. De ce nombre étaient Lafayette, Deprémesnil [*sic*], Sabathier etc. Il y avait une autre société moins nombreuse d'écrivains qui employaient leur plume à préparer cette révolution. C'était dans les dîners qu'on agitait les questions les plus importantes. J'y prêchais la république; mais, à l'exception de Clavière, personne ne la goûtait. Deprémesnil ne voulait *débourbonailler* la France (c'était son mot) que pour y faire régner le Parlement. Bergasse voulait un roi et les deux chambres, mais il voulait surtout faire le plan seul, et que ce plan fût rigoureusement exécuté: sa manie était de se croire un Lycurgue.

On ne peut disconvenir que les efforts de Bergasse et ceux de la société qui se rassemblait chez lui n'aient singulièrement contribué à accélérer la Révolution. On ne peut calculer toutes les brochures sorties de son sein. C'est de ce foyer que partirent presque tous les écrits publiés en 1787 et 1788 contre le ministère, et il faut rendre justice à Kornmann: il consacra une partie de sa fortune à ces publications. On en dut plusieurs à Gorsas, qui essayait alors la plume satirique avec laquelle il a si souvent déchiré le monarchisme, l'autocratie, le feuillantisme et l'anarchie. Carra se distinguait aussi dans ces combats, auxquels je pris quelque part.

Page 84   [Vous] exercez sans cesse le despotisme le plus complet dont l'homme soit capable . . . Vous devenez des souverains absolus chez le peuple malade.

On vous l'a dit cent fois: en criant contre le despotisme, vous en êtes les plus fermes appuis, vous en exercez vous-mêmes un révoltant.

Il importe d'y maintenir, comme un moyen constant de civilisation, tous les préjugés qui peuvent rendre la médecine respectable . . . Le corps des médecins est un corps politique, dont la destinée est liée avec celle de l'Etat . . . Ainsi dans l'ordre social, il nous faut absolument des maladies, des drogues et des lois, et les distributeurs des drogues et des maladies influent peut-être autant sur les habitudes d'une nation que les dépositaires des lois.

la politique de l'Etat, auquel il importe de conserver ces deux corps.

Page 85   la destruction de cette science fatale, la plus ancienne superstition de l'univers, de cette médecine tyrannique qui, saisissant l'homme dès le berceau, pèse sur lui comme un préjugé religieux.

Page 86   rappela l'autorité à sa circonspection et à sa prudence ordinaires; et dès ce moment le magnétisme et son auteur n'eurent plus de persécution publique à redouter.

En 1780 a commencé à Paris la vogue du magnétisme. La police avait à prendre sur cette pratique ancienne . . . par rapport à la pratique des moeurs . . . Le gouvernement n'y opposa [que] de l'indifférence pendant la vie de M. de Maurepas. Cependant quelque temps après sa mort, la police fut avertie par des lettres anonymes que l'on tenait dans les assemblées des magnétiseurs, des discours séditieux contre la religion et contre le gouvernement. L'un des ministres du Roi proposa alors sur la dénonciation de la police de renvoyer hors du royaume l'étranger Mesmer . . . D'autres ministres furent d'avis, et plus écoutés, que c'était au Parlement que devaient être poursuivies toutes sectes et assemblées illicites, immorales, irréligieuses. Je fus chargé de provoquer le procureur général. Ce magistrat me répondit que s'il portait sa plainte contre les assemblées du magnétisme à la Grande Chambre, elle serait renvoyée aux chambres assemblées où il se trouverait des partisans et protecteurs du magnétisme. Il ne fut donc aucune poursuite.

Page 88   Que pensera Washington quand il saura que vous êtes devenu le premier garçon apothicaire de Mesmer?

Un docteur allemand, nommé Mesmer, ayant fait la plus grande découverte sur le magnétisme animal, a formé des élèves, parmi lesquels votre humble serviteur est appelé l'un des plus enthousiastes.— J'en sais autant qu'un sorcier en sut jamais . . . Avant de partir, j'obtiendrai la permission de vous confier le secret de Mesmer, qui, vous pouvez y croire, est une grande découverte philosophique.

Page 89   On trouve du plaisir à descendre, tant qu'on croit
remonter dès qu'on veut; et, sans prévoyance, nous
goûtions tout à la fois les avantages du patriciat
et les douceurs d'une philosophie plébéienne.

Page 91   L'empire des sciences ne doit connaître ni despotes,
ni aristocrates, ni électeurs. Il offre l'image d'une
république parfaite. Là, le mérite est le seul titre
pour y être honoré. Admettre un despote, ou des
aristocrates, ou des électeurs ... c'est violer la nature
des choses, la liberté de l'esprit humain; c'est
attenter à l'opinion publique, qui seule a le droit
de couronner le génie; c'est introduire un despotisme révoltant.

Page 92   Vous savez, mon très cher, la place que vous occu-
pez dans mon coeur.

Les âmes franches et droites comme la vôtre ne
connaissent pas toutes les routes tortueuses des
satellites d'un despote, ou plutôt elles les dédaignent.

Page 94   On a besoin du zèle d'un ami quand on a à combattre une si puissante faction.

Je m'occuperai de M. Mesmer, et vous en rendrai
bon compte. Mais ce n'est pas l'affaire du moment.
Vous savez combien j'aime à examiner les choses,
et à les examiner avec soin avant de prononcer.

courageusement renversé l'idole du culte académique, et substitué au système de Newton sur la
lumière de faits bien prouvés.

Page 95   Je viens vous donner une leçon, Messieurs, j'en ai
le droit; je suis indépendant et il n'est aucun de
vous qui ne soit esclave: je ne tiens à aucun corps,
et vous tenez au vôtre; je ne tiens à aucun préjugé,
et vous êtes enchainés par ceux de votre corps, par
ceux de toutes les personnes en place que vous
révérez bassement comme des Idoles, quoique
vous les méprisez en secret.

Page 96   Un fait extraordinaire est un fait qui ne se lie point
à la chaîne de ceux que nous connaissons ou des
lois que nous avons fabriquées. Mais devons-nous
croire que nous les connaissons tous?

... portait le peuple, les malheureux dans son coeur.

Mais moi qui suis père et qui crains les médecins, j'aime le magnétisme parce qu'il m'identifie avec mes enfants. Quelle douceur pour moi . . . quand je les vois obéissants à ma voix intérieure, se courber, tomber dans mes bras et goûter le sommeil! L'état de mère nourrice est un état de magnétisme perpétuel. Nous pères infortunés que les affaires traînent, nous ne sommes presque rien pour nos enfants; par le magnétisme nous devenons pères encore une fois. Voilà donc un nouveau bien, créé dans la société, et elle en a tant besoin!

lueurs sublimes . . . au-delà de notre globe, dans un meilleur monde.

presque tous les vrais philosophes, et surtout Rousseau. Lisez ses Dialogues avec lui-même. Ils semblent écrits dans un autre monde. L'auteur qui n'existe que dans celui-ci, qui n'en a jamais franchi les limites, n'en écrirait pas deux phrases.

Page 97   Ne voyez-vous pas, par exemple, que le magnétisme est un moyen de rapprocher les états, de rendre les riches plus humains, d'en faire de vrais pères aux pauvres? Ne seriez-vous pas édifié en voyant des hommes du premier rang . . . veiller sur la santé de leurs domestiques, passer des heures entières à les magnétiser.

cherché à enflammer le gouvernement contre les partisans du magnétisme.

Je crains bien que l'habitude du despotisme n'ait ossifié vos âmes. bas parasites oppresseurs de la patrie viles adulateurs . . . des grands, des riches, des princes demi-talents qui se mettent perpétuellement en avant et repoussent le vrai talent qui se cache.

Si sur votre chemin se trouve un de ces hommes libres, indépendants . . . vous le louez, vous le plaignez, mais vous faites entendre que sa plume est dangereuse, que le gouvernement l'a proscrite, que sa proscription pouvait entraîner celle du journal.

pour de l'argent vous amusez donc les femmes de bon ton et les jeunes gens ennuyés qui prennent une leçon de littérature ou d'histoire comme une leçon de danse et d'escrime.

Page 98   C'est là surtout que vous avez déployé votre esprit d'intrigue, votre despotisme impérieux, vos manoeuvres auprès des grands et des femmes.

Page 99   C'est un génie créateur; il explique tout par la force centrifuge, jusqu'à l'odeur d'une fleur.

des absurdités et les rêveries d'un imbécile.

Excepté quelques hommes privilégiés de la nature et de la raison, les autres ne sont pas faits pour me comprendre.

des crocodiles monstrueux, vomissant des flammes de tous côtés: leurs yeux sont rouges de sang: ils tuent de leur seul regard.

Page 100 purger cette même terre des monstres qui la dévorent.

Page 101 d'ouvrir au mérite la voie des dignités, des honneurs.

Quel foyer puissant que celui de l'ambition! Heureux l'Etat où, pour être le premier, il ne faut qu'être le plus grand en mérite.

Il faut nous rendre notre liberté; il faut nous ouvrir toutes les carrières.

Page 102 On sait quelle est ma fortune, on n'ignore pas qu'elle me met au-dessus de toute espèce de besoins, qu'elle me rend absolument indépendant.

Avant qu'il ait plu à ce bon peuple de vouloir être libre, j'avais un capital de cinq à six mille livres de rente et de plus un intérêt dans la maison de mes frères me rapportant annuellement dix mille livres et devant par la suite me rapporter davantage.

Page 103 En général tous les privilèges exclusifs sont favorables à quelques genres d'aristocratie; il n'est que le Roi et le peuple dont l'intérêt constant soit général.

Il faut être bien antérieur au quatorzième siècle pour prétendre exercer près du trône cet aristocratisme qui détermine dans quel ordre le Roi doit choisir les serviteurs de sa maison et de son armée.

Page 104   En essayant ainsi d'ôter aux prétensions de l'antique aristocratie l'influence plus lucrative que le pouvoir passé, comment espérez vous réussir?

Vous n'aurez pour vous que la loi, le peuple et le Roi.

Page 108   Les mêmes effets ont lieu, à chaque instant, dans la société, et l'on ne s'est pas encore avisé, je pense, d'y attacher cette importance, parce qu'on n'a pas encore assez lié le moral au physique.

car le grand système physique de l'univers qui régit le système moral et politique du genre humain, est lui-même une véritable république.

Page 110   Celui-ci n'est plus un roi; celui-là est toujours un berger; ou pour mieux dire ceux ne sont plus que deux hommes dans le véritable état d'égalité, deux amis dans le véritable état de société. La différence politique a disparu . . . La nature, l'égalité ont réclamé tous leurs droits . . . C'est à vous, mes semblables, mes frères . . . à diriger, sur ce plan la marche de votre volonté particulière pour en conduire le résultat au centre du bonheur commun.

Le globe entier semble se préparer, par une révolution marquée dans la marche des saisons, à des changements physiques . . . La masse des sociétés s'agite, plus que jamais, pour débrouiller enfin le chaos de sa morale et de sa législation.

Page 111   Il affectait alors de porter la doctrine du magnétisme animal au plus haut degré d'illumination; il y voyait tout la médecine, la morale, l'économie politique, la philosophie, l'astronomie, le passé, le présent à toutes les distances et même le futur; tout cela ne remplissait que quelques facettes de sa vaste vision mesmérienne.

Il viendra sans doute un temps, où l'on sera convaincu que le grand principe de la santé physique est l'égalité entre tous les êtres, et l'indépendance des opinions et des volontés.

Page 112   Quand le plus fervent apôtre du magnétisme, M. Bergasse, a pulverisé votre rapport dans *ses profondes considérations,* vous avez dit: c'est une tête exaltée.

écraser l'homme de génie indépendant. Mais on le loue en le peignant ainsi, car dire qu'un homme est exalté, c'est dire que ses idées sortent de la sphère des idées ordinaires, qu'il a des vertus publiques sous un gouvernement corrompu, de l'humanité parmi des barbares, du respect pour les droits de l'homme sous le despotisme... Et tel est dans la vérité le portrait de M. Bergasse.

Page 113   une science nouvelle, celle de l'influence du moral sur le physique.

Quoi! ces phénomènes physiques et moraux que j'admire tous les jours sans les comprendre, ont pour cause le même agent... Tous les êtres sont donc mes frères et la nature n'est donc qu'une mère commune!

Page 114   qui s'unit par des fibres aussi nombreuses que déliées à tous les points de l'univers... C'est par cet organe que nous nous mettons en harmonie avec la nature.

des règles simples pour juger les institutions auxquelles nous sommes asservis, des principes certains pour constituer la législation qui convient à l'homme dans toutes les circonstances données.

Page 115   Rien ne s'accorde mieux avec les notions que nous nous sommes faites d'un Etre suprême, rien ne prouve plus sa sagesse profonde, que le monde formé en conséquence d'une idée unique, mû par une seule loi.

L'attraction est une vertu occulte, une propriété inhérente, on ne sait comment, dans la matière.

Il existe un principe incréé: Dieu. Il existe dans la Nature deux principes créés: la matière et le mouvement.

Le magnétisme animal, entre les mains de M. Mesmer, ne paraît autre chose que la nature même.

Page 116   Il en résulte que le mouvement est imprimé par Dieu, ce qui est incontestable et une réponse aussi simple que forte contre l'athéisme.

Page 117   Je m'y sentais plus près de la nature... O nature, m'écriais-je dans ces accès, que me veux-tu?

transmettre à l'humanité dans toute la pureté que je l'avais reçu de la Nature, le bienfaisant inappréciable que j'avais en main.

Sans cesse ils insistaient sur la félicité des premiers ages, sur les préjugés, la corruption du monde actuel, sur la nécessité d'une révolution, d'une réforme générale.

Page 118   Nos propos ont eté plus graves lorsqu'il s'est jeté sur l'article des moeurs et de la constitution actuelle des gouvernements . . . Nous touchons, a-t-il ajouté, à quelque grande révolution.

Vous n'êtes pas la première qui m'ayez trouvé quelques ressemblances avec votre bon ami Jean-Jacques. Seulement il y a quelques principes qu'il n'a pas connus, et qui l'eussent rendu moins malheureux.

Par le mot société il ne faut pas entendre la société telle qu'elle existe maintenant . . . mais la société telle qu'elle doit être, la société naturelle, celle qui résulte des rapports que notre organisation bien ordonnée doit produire . . . La règle de la société est l'harmonie.

M. Bergasse pour parler de la constitution et des droits de l'homme, nous faisait remonter aux temps de la Nature, à l'état sauvage.

Page 120   Tout changement, toute altération dans notre constitution physique, produisent donc infailliblement un changement, une altération dans notre constitution morale. Il ne faut donc quelquefois qu'épurer ou corrompre le régime physique d'une nation pour opérer une révolution dans ses moeurs.

Page 121   Nous devons à nos institutions presque tous les maux physiques auxquels nous sommes en proie.

Nous n'appartenons presque plus à la nature . . . L'enfant qui naît aujourd'hui appartenant à une organisation modifiée depuis plusieurs siècles par les habitudes . . . de la société, doit toujours porter en lui des germes de dépravation plus ou moins considérables.

C'est surtout à la campagne et dans la classe de la société la plus malheureuse et la moins dépravée que seront d'abord recueillis les fruits de la découverte que j'ai faite; c'est là qu'il est aisé de replacer l'homme sous l'empire des lois conservatrices de la nature.

L'homme du peuple, l'homme qui vit aux champs, quand il est malade, guérit plus vite et mieux que l'homme qui vit dans le monde.

Page 122   En harmonie avec lui-même, avec tout ce qui l'environne, il se déploie dans la nature, si l'on peut se servir de ce terme, et c'est le seul terme dont on puisse se servir ici, comme l'arbrisseau qui étend des fibres vigoureuses dans un sol fécond et facile.

Page 123   l'indépendance primitive dans laquelle la Nature nous a fait naître.

un moyen d'énerver l'espèce humaine, de la réduire à n'avoir que le degré de force nécessaire pour porter avec docilité le joug des institutions sociales.

Page 124   une institution qui appartient autant à la politique qu'à la nature.

Si par hasard le magnétisme animal existait . . . à quelle révolution, je vous le demande, Monsieur, ne faudrait-il pas nous attendre? Lorsqu'à notre génération épuisée par des maux de toute espèce et par les remèdes inventés pour la délivrer de ces maux, succéderait une génération hardie, vigoureuse, et qui ne connaîtrait d'autres lois pour se conserver, que celles de la Nature: que deviendraient nos habitudes, nos arts, nos coutumes . . . Une organisation plus robuste nous rappelerait à l'indépendance; quand avec une autre constitution, il nous faudrait d'autre moeurs, . . . comment pourrions nous supporter le joug des institutions qui nous régissent aujourd'hui?

Page 131   que la révolution politique de la France est purement initiatoire d'une révolution religieuse, morale, politique et universelle dans toute la terre.

Les sectes d'illuminés augmentent, au lieu de diminuer; peut-être n'est-ce qu'un résultat des circonstances politiques de la France, qui rallie à leur doctrine mystérieuse les hommes mécontents du nouvel ordre des choses, et qui espèrent y trouver des moyens de le détruire.

Page 132   Dieu est le cerveau matériel et intellectuel du grand animal unique, du Tout, dont l'intelligence est un fluide réel, comme la lumière, mais encore plus subtil, puisqu'il ne contacte aucun de nos sens externes, et qu'il n'agit que sur le sens intérieur.

Page 133   répandre enfin les principes de cette divine harmonie qui doit faire concerter la Nature avec la Société.

Leur force motrice, cachée, fondamentale, vous apprendra que la *parole libre* et *pure,* image ardente de la vérité, saura tout éclairer par sa chaleur active, tout *aimanter* par sa puissance *attractive, électriser* d'excellents *conducteurs, organiser* les hommes, les nations et l'univers.

Page 134   Quelle est cette harpe divine, entre les mains du Dieu de la nature, dont les cordes universelles, attachées à tous les coeurs, les lient et les relient sans cesse? C'est la vérité. Aux plus faibles sons qui lui échappent toutes les nations deviennent attentives, tout ressent la divine influence de l'harmonie universelle.

Page 137   Telle est, mes amis, la doctrine que je voulais vous exposer avant de mourir . . . Telle est *ma Religion* . . . et je permettrai aux tyrans d'envoyer ma *monade* se prosterner devant l'ETERNEL. Valete et me amate. 10 juin 1793.

Page 138   Le fluide magnétique n'est autre chose que l'homme universel lui-même, ému et mis en mouvement par une de ses émanations.

Ce qu'il y a de plus bizarre, c'est que le général Bonaparte partant pour sa première campagne d'Italie, voulut se faire prédire, par le somnambuliste Mally-Châteaurenaud le sort qui l'attendait à l'armée . . . Bonaparte crut que la bataille de Castiglione réalisait la prédiction du somnambuliste qu'il fit rechercher avec soin avant son départ pour l'Egypte.

Page 143   Il faut jeter au feu toutes les théories politiques, morales et économiques, et se préparer à l'événement le plus étonnant . . . AU PASSAGE SUBIT DU CHAOS SOCIAL A L'HARMONIE UNIVERSELLE.

Je reconnus bientôt que les lois de l'Attraction
passionnée étaient en tout point conformes à celles
de l'Attraction matérielle, expliquées par Newton
et Leibnitz, et qu'il y avait UNITE DE SYSTEME
DE MOUVEMENT POUR LE MONDE MATERIEL
ET POUR LE MONDE SPIRITUEL.

Page 144   Mais si la découverte est l'ouvrage d'un inconnu,
d'un provincial ou paria scientifique, d'un de ces
intrus qui ont comme Prion le tort de n'être pas
même académiciens, il doit encourir tous les ana-
thèmes de la cabale.

Page 145   M. VINAQUIN—Assurément. Demandez à la
table, c'est-à-dire à l'esprit qui est dedans; il vous
dira que j'ai au-dessus de la tête un tuyau immense
de fluide qui monte de mes cheveuz jusqu'auz
astres; c'est une *trompe aromale* par laquèle la voiz
des esprits de Saturne vient jusqu'à mon oreille . . .
LA TABLE (frapant vivement du pié)—Oui, oui,
oui. Trompe aromale. Canal. Trompe aromale.
Canal. Canal. Canal. Canal. Oui. (Erdan's peculiar
spelling is retained here.)

Page 146   M. Owen, le socialiste célèbre . . . qui a été jusqu'ici
matérialiste dans toute la force du mot, a été par-
faitement converti à la croyance de l'immortalité
par les conversations qu'il a eues avec des personnes
de sa famille mortes depuis des années.

que l'objet des manifestations générales actuelles
est de réformer la population de notre planète, de
nous convaincre tous de la vérité d'une autre vie,
de nous rendre tous sincèrement charitables.

Page 147   Il sera prouvé enfin, par les principes qui forment
le système des influences ou du magnétisme animal,
combien il est important pour l'harmonie physique
et morale de l'homme de s'assembler fréquemment
en sociétés nombreuses . . . où toutes les intentions
et les volontés soient dirigées vers un et même
objet, surtout vers l'ordre de la nature, en chantant,
en priant ensemble; et que c'est dans ces situations
que l'harmonie qui commence à se troubler dans
quelques individus peut se rétablir et que la santé
se raffermit.

Page 148   Nos savants ne voulaient point de magnétisme, comme d'autres hommes point de liberté . . . [mais] les anneaux de la chaîne despotique que la science n'avait point voulu rompre ont volé en éclats.

Réjouissez-vous magnétiseurs, voici l'aurore d'un bel et grand jour . . . O Mesmer! toi qui aimais la république . . . tu pressentais les temps; mais . . . tu ne fus point compris.

Page 150   La science n'est donc pas un vain mot comme la vertu! Mesmer a vaincu Brutus.

Page 151   le fantastique, le mystérieux, l'occulte, l'inexplicable.

Voltaire, des Encyclopédistes tombe; qu'on se lasse enfin de tout, surtout de raisonner froidement; qu'il faut des jouissances plus vives, plus délicieuses, du sublime, de l'incompréhensible, du surnaturel.

Page 153   Il voulait être un grand homme et il le fut par d'incessantes projections de ce fluide plus puissant que l'électricité, et dont il fait de si subtiles analyses dans *Louis Lambert*.

Page 154   Il existe un fluide magnétique très subtil, lien chez l'homme entre l'âme et le corps; sans siège particulier, il circule dans tous les nerfs qu'il tend et détend au gré de la volonté. Il est l'esprit de la vie; sa couleur est celle de l'étincelle électrique . . . les regards, ces rayonnements de l'esprit de vie, sont la chaîne mystérieuse qui, à travers l'espace, relie sympathiquement les âmes.

La volonté, nous disait un jour H. de Balzac, est la force motrice du fluide impondérable, et les membres en sont les agents conducteurs.

la doctrine de Mesmer, qui reconnaissait en l'homme l'existence d'une influence pénétrante . . . mise en oeuvre par la volonté, curative par l'abondance du fluide.

Le magnétisme animal, aux miracles duquel je me suis familiarisé depuis 1820; les belles recherches de Gall, le continuateur de Lavater, tous ceux qui depuis cinquante ans ont travaillé la pensée comme les opticiens ont travaillé la lumière, deux choses quasi semblables, concluent et pour les mystiques, ces disciples de l'apôtre Saint Jean, et pour les grands penseurs qui ont établi le monde spirituel.

Page 156   fluide insaisissable, base des phénomènes de la volonté humaine, et d'où résultent les passions, les habitudes, les formes du visage et du crâne.

Page 157   la science, sous prétexte de merveillosité, s'est soustraite au devoir scientifique, qui est de tout approfondir.

Page 162   Sur terre je vous respectais, mais ici nous sommes égaux.

Page 164   S'il faut être jugé, que ce soit donc par un public éclairé et impartial: c'est à son tribunal que j'en appelle avec confiance, ce tribunal suprême dont les corps scientifiques eux-mêmes sont forcés de respecter les arrêts.

C'est au public que j'en appelle.

Page 165   Paris est plein de jeunes gens qui prennent quelque facilité pour du talent, de clercs, commis, avocats, militaires, qui se font auteurs, meurent de faim, mendient même, et font des brochures.

INDEX

Académie Française, 41
Academy of Medicine, 141
Academy of Sciences: and anti-mesmerist movement, 48, 62, 83; and Marat, 93, 94; and Carra, 99; mentioned, 17, 20, 22, 28, 29, 113, 161
Alael, 33
Alchemy, 12, 33–34, 68, 70, 127
Alembert, J-B. LeRond d', 59
Alexander I, Tsar of Russia, 139–140
Allonville, comte d', 138
American Philosophical Society, 91
American Revolution, 41, 88, 110
Animalculism, see Preformation theory
Artois, C. P. de Bourbon, comte d', 48
Assembly of Notables, 41, 42, 163
Avignon, 31

Bacon, Sir Francis, 39
Bailly, J. S., 11, 38, 62, 113, 118, 148n
Ballanche, Pierre, 142–143
Balloon flights, 10, 18–22, 41, 162
Balzac, Honoré de, 150, 153–157; Gautier on, 152–153
Barbaroux, C. J. M., 28
Barberin, chevalier de, 68, 69
Barruel, abbé, 73, 131, 163
Bastille, 83, 97, 105
Bayle, Pierre, 39
Bayonne, 52, 58
Bergasse, Nicolas: and Society of Harmony, 51–52, 75–78, 112, 114, 180–182; and Kornmann group, 72, 78–80; lectures on mesmerism, 76–77, 183–185; defense of mesmerism, 84–87; wealth, 101–102; anti-aristocratic convictions, 103–104;

political ideas, 112–125, 146, 147; and Rousseau, 117–118; and Duchesse de Bourbon, 128, 130; and Tsar Alexander I, 139–140; mentioned, 3, 44, 47, 70, 83, 96, 163, 166
Bergerac, 74
Berkeley, Bishop George, 11
Bernardin de Saint-Pierre, Henri, 12
Berthollet, Claude, comte, 52
Bertholon, abbé, 14, 39
Besançon, 66
Bibliothèque du Roi, 100
Black, Joseph, 16
Blackwell, Anna, 146
Bléton, 31, 96
Boehme, Jacob, 12
Boerhaave, Herman, 18
Bonnet, Charles, 13, 39
Bonneville, Nicolas de, 133–135
Bordeaux, 22, 52, 58, 70, 74
Boston, 28
Bottineau, 96
Bourbon, duchesse de, 70, 128–130, 139, 149
Braid, James, 142
Breteuil, L. A. Le Tonnelier, baron de, 42
Brienne, E. C. Loménie de, 88, 123, 163
Brissot de Warville, J.-P.: and Kornmann group, 79, 95, 100; prerevolutionary radicalism, 83, 88, 91–98, 111–112, 163–167; attack on academicians, 84; and Marat, 92–94; defense of mesmerism, 95–98, 104; antimesmerist after Revolution, 130–131; and Cercle Social, 134, 135; mentioned, 3, 32, 44, 111, 146
Buffon, G. L. Leclerc, comte de, 11, 12, 14, 39, 59
Buzancy, 58